TORTURED MINDS

Pennsylvania's most bizarre—but forgotten—murders

Tammy Mal

ALSO BY TAMMY MAL;

LITTLE GIRL LOST: THE TRUE STORY OF THE VANDLING MURDER

DISPOSABLE INCOME: A TRUE STORY OF SEX, GREED AND IM-PURR-FECT MURDER

For Dave:

My best friend and biggest supporter.

AUTHORS NOTE

The four stories you are about to read are some of the strangest I have ever encountered. Some people kill because their minds are tortured, some simply because they enjoy it, and others for no apparent reason at all. Each of these cases made headlines when they occurred, but, as far as I can tell, none of them has ever been written about in detail.

Researching such old crimes is difficult. Few witnesses involved in the events are still living, and I had little choice but to rely heavily on newspaper articles and some court documents. Many of the details were taken directly from the killers' own confessions. Whenever possible, if the perpetrator's recall did not match that of their victim or a witness, both versions have been provided.

The reader should be warned that some parts of this book are extremely graphic. When dealing with true crime the events can be horrific and hard to read, but in order to be accurate they need to be told as they occurred.

Some pseudonyms have been included in the book, and will be identified on first use by an asterisk, (*).

I owe a big thank you to the following people:
Regge Episale, my editor, for all her time and dedication, and whose help was invaluable to this project.
Sherry Sparks, one of the most talented photographers I've ever had the pleasure to know, and who did such a terrific job on the cover design for the book.
My family, Tim, Ian, Tyler and Shauna, who are always neglected when I write.
The Keim family, who are going through their own nightmare as we speak.
And of course, my loyal readers who make it all worthwhile.

THE LOVE CULT OF 1931

(Wilkes-Barre, PA. The murder of spinster Minnie Dilley)

Anning Dilley hurried along River Street on that blustery, cold day, one hand clutching the lapel of his overcoat, the other clamped firmly upon his hat which was threatening to blow away at any moment. The gusty breeze from the river was biting and icy, and he walked with his head bent in an effort to shield his face from it. He was miserable at the moment, and silently cursing the God-awful weather. It was Saturday, April 4, 1931, supposedly spring in Northeastern Pennsylvania, but there was no sign of it in the air today.

Anning, a civil engineer who worked in the city of Wilkes-Barre, should have been on his way home to a dry and cozy house where a warm fire waited. Instead, at the urging of a relative, he found himself bracing against a hurricane wind, and hurrying to check on his Aunt Minnie.

Normally, Anning wouldn't have minded this task, but he had a lot of work to do tonight and found this unexpected glitch in his plans somewhat annoying. Tomorrow was Easter Sunday, and there were still preparations to be made. He couldn't help thinking that this would turn out to be a waste of time anyway, that his Aunt Minnie would be perfectly fine. He knew she was sometimes eccentric, and she *was,* after all, old; if she hadn't answered the phone, it was probably because she'd been napping, or simply hadn't heard it.

Still though, Anning's relative had sounded highly concerned when she told him Minnie hadn't been heard from in *days,* and he knew that was unusual. His aunt was a seventy-six-year-old spinster who rarely left her palatial house on the banks of the Susquehanna River, in the ritzy historic district of the small town of Forty Fort. Minnie's relatives worried about her living all alone in that big old house and made it a habit to regularly check on her. What if she fell and broke a bone? Or got sick and couldn't get to the phone?

There was something else that concerned them about the old woman living all alone, something everyone in town was aware of. Minnie Dilley was rich. A descendant of one of Wyoming County's oldest pioneering families, Minnie had been a shrewd businesswoman all her life. She had no children (in fact had never married), had amassed a small fortune in her years of business, and was the owner of several rental properties (a rarity for a single woman in those days). She was, so it seemed, a woman far ahead of her time, and at seventy-six, a potentially easy target for burglars. As these thoughts drifted through Anning's mind, his annoyance began to wane and he instinctively quickened his pace.

Finally arriving at the house, Anning hesitated for a moment, as he always did when he saw Aunt Minnie's "mansion." The house, an old Victorian with gabled roofs and narrow windows was somehow sinister, even foreboding. It wasn't *how* the house looked that spooked the man so much, however, it was the way his Aunt had transformed it into a literal fortress. Each window was screwed shut on the inside and heavily shuttered on the out, each door enhanced with solid iron bars and deadbolt locks, and throughout the entire structure, strategically placed peep holes had been drilled. Apparently Minnie Dilley's family weren't the only ones concerned about burglars.

As Anning gazed at the house now, he felt a nagging sensation in the pit of his stomach; a vague feeling that something wasn't right, and suddenly it hit him. Minnie Dilley's house stood in complete darkness. No thin beam of light streamed through any of the shutters, no warm glow seeped from beneath the doors. The house was black, silent, and seemingly dead.

The house being in darkness gave Anning Dilley his first real hint of alarm. He knew his aunt never went out at night, and although it was already dark, it certainly wasn't late; and far too early for her to be in bed.

The worried man rang the bell several times, listening for movement inside. When he heard nothing, he switched to knocking, pounding on the door so hard it rattled the thin-paned window that adorned it. Again, however, no sound came from within.

The door was locked, as he knew it would be, and peering through the barred window was impossible; it was far too dark inside to see anything. Anning stood there for a moment, frightened and unsure of what to do. Then, noticing a light in a neighbor's house, he hurried to it.

~*~*~

Minnie Dilley's neighbor, Catherine Defoe*, had noticed the hesitant young man standing outside, gazing up at Minnie's house. She watched as he eventually went to the door, knocked loudly, and then tried to open it. Soon, the man disappeared from sight, and shortly after she saw the beam of a flashlight shining around in Minnie's backyard.

Worried that a break-in was occurring, Catherine immediately called another neighbor, Dave Evans*, and explained what she had seen Would Evans go over and investigate, she asked, and check on Minnie Dilley?

Dave Evans, concerned, but having no desire to interrupt a burglar who might have a weapon, hung up the phone and called the police. Chief A.J. Klinger took the call and immediately assigned Patrolman Sutliff to go check it out.

Meanwhile, Anning Dilley, having borrowed a flashlight from Minnie's neighbor, found he was still unable to peer through any of his aunt's windows. Going around to the back of the house, he discovered a side door which was locked, but not dead-bolted—a finding that greatly upset him. Anning knew his aunt would never have been so careless as to forget to set the deadbolt.

Reluctant, but feeling he had no choice, Anning put his shoulder to the door, and, using all his weight, forced the lock and stepped inside. The first thing he noticed was how cold it was. There had obviously been no fire burning for quite some time. He hesitated, suddenly becoming aware of how truly terrified he was. His heart was beating wildly in his chest and, despite the chill, he was sweating profusely. He called out his aunt's name, listening as his voice echoed in the vast emptiness of the house, but there was no reply, no sound at all. He was afraid to turn on any lights, so instead, began to inch his way by the beam of the flashlight.

Minnie Dilley's house was huge, old fashioned, and eerily silent. Other than the tick-tock of the grandfather clock located in the entryway at the base of the Mahogany stairs, the house was as still as a grave. The sound of the clock was somehow disconcerting, seeming to magnify with every moment that ticked by.

The darkness was impenetrable, the dim glow of the flashlight barely cutting through the gloom. As he made his way from the kitchen through the hallway, he could see, up ahead, the entrance to the living room. Anning knew that directly in front of him stood a large stone fireplace which customarily contained a roaring fire, but tonight the room was pitch black.

As he approached, he tentatively moved the flashlight back and forth, illuminating glimpses of furniture, antiques, and ornately framed paintings, until the swatch of light came to rest on a shocking scene. There, on the living room floor, directly in front of the elaborate stone fireplace, lay the body of his Aunt Minnie, crumpled in a heap, covered in blood.

Anning Dilley stopped short; his mind reeling. His body trembled with fear as he gazed at his fallen aunt and the splashes of red that drenched the room. He seemed unable to look away as his mind tried to comprehend what he was seeing. Finally, he turned and ran back along the passageway crashing through the side door he had so recently forced open. He didn't look behind as he rushed down River Street. In fact, he was so distraught that he didn't even notice the Forty Fort patrol car that raced past him, headed in the direction of his aunt's house.

~*~*~

A.J. Klinger, chief of the Forty Fort Police, was sitting at his desk going over some paperwork when the station door burst open, and Anning Dilley hurried in. Glancing around fretfully, he spotted the chief and rushed over to him.

"My aunt's been killed!" he shouted. "You have to do something!"

Chief Klinger noted that the man was near panic and tried to put him at ease. "Hold on son," he said, "Just take it easy." He gestured towards a chair before his desk. "Take a seat, and tell me what happened."

Anning willed himself to calm down, and, once composed, dropped into a leather chair facing the chief. When he spoke, he enunciated each word. "My aunt, Minnie Dilley, over on River Street, is lying dead in her living room."

The man's words caused the chief to sit up straighter in his chair. He had just sent Patrolman Sutliff to investigate a prowler on River Street, which was only about a block away.

"What makes you think she's dead?" He asked slowly.

"Because I saw her!" Anning yelled, rising in his seat a bit. "She's laying in the living room and there's blood all over."

Chief Klinger knew Minnie Dilley. Hell, everyone in Forty Fort knew her, and if she were lying dead on her living room floor, he figured it had to be from natural causes. Crime was rare in his small town, and Minnie Dilley's house was as secure as Fort Knox. Despite the fact that her nephew was insisting there was blood all over, Klinger couldn't imagine that someone had actually killed the old woman.

"I just sent an officer over to your aunt's house," the chief now told Anning. "We got a call about an intruder with a flashlight looking in the window."

"That wasn't an intruder," Anning said, "It was me. I borrowed a flashlight from a neighbor, and then forced a door to get inside."

"What exactly did you see?"

Minnie Dilley's nephew settled back in his chair and sighed. "Not much," he admitted. "I was scared. But I saw her on the floor in front of the fireplace, and I saw blood. No one in the family has heard from her in several days and they were worried. That's why I was coming to check on her."

At that moment, the phone in the station house began to shrill, and Chief Klinger picked it up immediately. It was Patrolman Sutliff, who told his boss that he had better get out to the Dilley house at once.

~*~*~

The scene at the Dilley mansion was horrific, gruesome, and shocking. The seventy-six-year-old spinster lay in a heap on her parlor floor; her face battered beyond recognition, her head nearly severed from her body. Blood, already cold, coagulated, and dry pooled around her limp body and splashed across the granite stone of her massive fireplace. There was a putrid smell to the corpse, a lingering odor of decay that made it clear the woman had not died recently, but had been dead for at least a day, and possibly two.

Near the body lay a full glass bottle of ginger ale, spattered with blood and obviously the weapon used to bludgeon the old woman's face and head. The jagged gash that had nearly decapitated her looked like it had been made by either an axe or a hacksaw, but there was no sign of either instrument anywhere in the room.

The house was neat and tidy, and appeared in immaculate condition. Other than the chaos right there in the narrow space before the fireplace, there were no visible signs of a struggle, and no indication that anything was missing. Valuable antiques lay undisturbed in plain sight, and on an end table near the settee rested a ten dollar bill and two fives. Why, the police wondered, would anyone want to kill the aged spinster if not to rob her? There were no signs of a break-in—other than the door that Anning Dilley admitted to forcing—which led police to believe that Minnie Dilley must have known her killer and willingly allowed him or her into the house.

After the old woman's body was removed to the morgue, the Forty Fort police did a cursory search of the house. After a short time, Chief Klinger told most of his men to go home and report back in the morning. It was getting late, and Klinger thought it'd be easier to investigate in the light of day. Before leaving, he posted a guard at the house and then gathered his men together and apologized to them. He was sorry, the chief said, but they would not be spending Easter with their families this year.

~*~*~

By daybreak, on the morning of April 5, 1931, police began a thorough search of Minnie Dilley's house. It was a daunting task, and one that would take several days to complete. The house was huge, and Minnie Dilley collected a lot of things. There were knick-knacks and figurines, glassware, bottles, jewelry, music boxes, and hundreds and hundreds of books. Thin volumes and thick, hardcovers, softcovers, leather-bound tomes and complete series; row upon row of every book imaginable.

While the Forty Fort officers worked inside the house, others, including several county detectives, began canvassing the River Street neighborhood. Many of those living nearby had their Easter dinners interrupted when police officers knocked on their doors, but few had much to tell.

One neighbor recalled that she had last seen Minnie on Tuesday, five days earlier, when the old woman had come outside to get her mail. Another neighbor thought she had seen the spinster on Thursday or Friday of that week, but couldn't be sure. Several others told investigators that there had been an unusually large number of tramps and beggars in the neighborhood over the past few weeks, something that they found uncommon and suspicious.

Although any tips received would have to be checked out, police were already developing a theory for the crime. The fact that Minnie had likely known her killer led some to consider revenge as a possible motive for the crime. Minnie had been a shrewd businesswoman most of her life. Was it possible she had made enemies during those dealings? Or, might one of her relatives have asked for a loan and been refused? Either seemed like a plausible scenario, and when police learned that Minnie Dilley had left an estate in excess of $50,000 they began to look at her relatives much more closely. Who would benefit from Minnie Dilley's death? Who was the beneficiary of her will?

Minnie Dilley's business associates were quickly eliminate suspects; the old woman had made most of her money from stocks a.. dealings that would create enemies. The financial angle as concerned her relatives excited the investigators at first, but this, too, led nowhere. They could find no family members who were having financial difficulties, none that appeared on bad terms with the old woman, and nobody who didn't seem genuinely shocked and grieved by her death. When they also learned that the bulk of Minnie's estate had been left to charity—a fact her family was well aware of—they soon abandoned that theory as a motive. No one in law enforcement was disappointed by this turn of events, because by then, they had already made a startling discovery in Minnie's mansion that would shift the investigation in an entirely new direction.

~*~*~

Authorities were being extremely secretive about the Dilley investigation, a fact that the press found maddeningly frustrating. They needed something to print, and when they heard a rumor that officers had found a highly detailed diary in the spinster's mansion they made a mad dash to get the story out. Two days later, on April 7th, when police insinuated that they knew who the killer was and expected to make an arrest shortly, the press took this as confirmation, and re-ran the diary story, hinting that the killer's name had been revealed in the book.

On April 8th, police made a trip to Pittsburgh where they took into custody thirty-three-year-old Carl Thomsen, a mild-mannered man who worked as a regional representative for the western district of a local lumber company. Learning that Luzerne County authorities had made an arrest in the Dilley case— an arrest 300 miles away—the press was quick to report the case as solved.

The case, however, was not solved, and much to the media's chagrin, the police released Carl Thomsen less than twenty-four hours after they had picked him up. Incredibly, the very next day, they arrested and charged someone else with Minnie's murder; Thomsen's twenty-nine-year-old wife, Frances.

Frances Thomsen seemed an unlikely suspect. Young, shy and timid, she was a junior high school teacher, and the mother of three small children: Frances, eight, Carl Jr., seven, and little Elvira, not yet two-years-old. She was the daughter of a Baptist minister, a graduate of the exclusive all-girls Wellesley College and a married woman for the past eleven years. It seemed unbelievable to the local press that such a meek and mild person—a woman—could be guilty of the brutal bludgeoning and near decapitation of Minnie Dilley.

Of course, the police had been very tight-lipped about their investigation and hadn't felt the need to inform the press that they had not found a diary in Minnie Dilley's house. What they had found, however, tucked away in her upstairs bedroom, was a stack of more than 100 letters. Bizarre in nature, the correspondence was filled with incoherent ramblings containing both pleas for Minnie Dilley and threats against her. In some of the letters, the writer had begged to come and live with the aged spinster, and in others the author's tone became sinister and threatening. Each letter bore the return address of Thomsen, 1920 Fifth St., Pittsburgh, PA, and all had been signed Frances. The letters spanned a three-year period, the last one dated March 31, 1931, only four days before the brutalized body of Minnie Dilley was found.

When shown the threatening letters, Minnie's family admitted that they were aware of them, although they had not known just how prolific the writing campaign had become.

Minnie's sister-in-law told investigators that the first letter Frances Thomsen had sent had not gone to Minnie, but to herself. Retrieving the missive, she gave it to the police who noted that it was mailed from Hollis, Long Island, and dated March 5, 1929. The letter was written in the same vein as all the others, a rambling, panic-stricken, incoherent plea for help. In part, it read, *"You must help me to put an end to Minnie's efforts to win my husband away from me. She is destroying my life and my family. We must combat the strange influence she is exerting over my husband, and I am asking for your help to do so."*

The police wanted to know what connection Frances Thomsen had to Minnie Dilley, and learned that years earlier the two families had been neighbors. In fact, up until four years ago, Carl and Frances had rented a house from Minnie, located right across the street from her own on River Street. Minnie had been happy to have them as tenants; her relatives said since the Thomsen's appeared to be fine people who were well-known and highly respected around town.

Frances was teaching English at Latimer Junior High in Forty Fort, and was also a member of the local branch of the Wellesley College Alumnae Association. Her husband, Carl, was working as a salesman for a large lumber company, and was considered something of a genius when it came to electrical lines. In fact, he had maintained a radio laboratory in his basement while the family lived on River Street, and had even hooked up a radio in Minnie's house for the old woman's listening pleasure.

Frances Thomsen was an articulate and cultured woman, Minnie's family asserted; a sophisticated lady who had no trouble socializing on Minnie Dilley's level. Over the years, the two had become quite close, spending many evenings together visiting in Minnie's mansion, where they would talk about literature, antiques, art, and books they had each read.

Both landlord and tenant seemed to have a wonderful relationship and appeared on good terms for many years, and then suddenly it was all over. Something had happened between Frances and Minnie that caused their friendship to cool markedly, although no one was certain of what it was. Shortly after the two women stopped being friends, however, the Thomsen's had moved away from Forty Fort, to Hollis, Long Island.

Frances had originally hailed from Pittsburgh, where her father, F.T. Galpin, had once been the minister of the First Baptist Church. Galpin had since left the clergy, however, and moved to Long Island to sell real estate. When the Thomsen's first left Forty Fort four years earlier, they had gone to Hollis to be near Frances' parents, and then later moved back to Pittsburgh because of Carl's work.

The letters found in the mansion were highly incriminating, but they were not the only evidence police had uncovered linking Frances Thomsen to the murder of Minnie Dilley. During their canvas of the River Street neighborhood, they had discovered several witnesses who thought they had seen Frances loitering near the Dilley house on Friday, the day before the body was discovered. Frances had lived on the street and was easily recognizable, plus, all of the witnesses said the woman they had seen walked with a distinct limp, which Frances did. And then, of course, there was the story her husband had to tell.

Carl Thomsen was a polite, short man, portly and balding, who wore wire-rimmed spectacles upon a moon shaped face. He looked distraught and upset when initially brought in, as well as visibly nervous. Luzerne County Assistant District Attorney Donald Coughlin, along with County Detective John Dempsey, and Sergeant Norman Anning of the Pennsylvania State Police, Troop B, each introduced themselves to the worried man and tried to put him at ease. Did he want any coffee or a soda, they asked? But Carl Thomsen, appearing eager to get this over with, answered no, that he was fine.

After explaining to him why they were there and the events surrounding Minnie Dilley's death, Coughlin asked Carl if he could shed any light on the matter. At first, Carl denied knowing anything about the crime, or anyone who might have reason to want his old landlady dead. But when Coughlin placed in front of him the stack of letters written to Minnie by his wife, Carl Thomsen covered his face with his hands and began to cry.

"My wife has been mentally ill for the past three years," Carl said, finally dropping his hands from his face to look his interrogators in the eye. "You have to understand, she was a model mother to the three children—a wonderful mother—but she was insanely jealous of me."

"What do you mean by that, 'insanely jealous of you?'" Coughlin asked.

"Well," Carl began, "if I went to a movie and a woman sat next to me, Frances would get up and leave the show. Or if we went out to play bridge and I had a woman guest as a partner she was suspicious. It didn't matter who the woman was. Whether she was old or young, pretty or ugly, fat or skinny, it didn't matter; Frances was jealous. She was jealous of Minnie Dilley, and she was even jealous of my male friends. This was bad enough, but things got even worse when she started receiving strange messages out of the air."

The three interviewers glanced at each other, remembering the strange writings that had been included in Frances Thomsen's letters to Minnie.

"My wife has been ill for years," Carl continued, "and has heard strange voices for all that time. But about six months ago, she started talking about Miss Dilley forming some type of love cult, and she said I was destined to be the leader of it."

He shook his head in bewilderment, as if still unable to believe the absurdity of it. "She said it was a cult which would give old women new youth, and that Miss Dilley would be the financier of it and was planning to move to New York to establish it."

Although those in the room kept their expressions bland, they were already well aware of the "love cult" that Frances Thomsen believed Minnie Dilley was forming. Almost every letter the young school teacher had written mentioned it, as well as the fact that Frances was not going to let her husband become the "high priest" of this "sinister love cult," which was what Minnie Dilley supposedly wanted.

"Frances thought Miss Dilley was exerting some type of influence over me," Carl said. "That she was in love with me and trying to steal me away from Frances and break up our family. My wife believed Miss Dilley was a witch who had cast a spell upon me. Frances is a big believer in witchcraft, despite the fact that she grew up in the church. Her father's a minister, you know."

The three investigators nodded their heads, acknowledging that they were aware of this, and then county detective Dempsey asked, "Do you honestly believe your wife heard voices?"

Carl nodded confidently. "I know Frances firmly believed in messages she got from strange voices in the air. She had been hearing these voices for two or three years, and I tried to tell her she was letting a voice out of the air spoil her life, but she wouldn't listen to me."

Carl went on to say that as the regional representative for the lumber company where he worked, his job required him to travel at times. For months now, whenever he'd come home from one of these trips, he'd find Frances crying and upset, accusing him of being in cahoots with Minnie Dilley. He'd deny it, of course, but his wife would not be placated. She claimed that the voices had told her of telephone conversations he had with their old landlord while he was away, and that it was Minnie Dilley's intention for him to head a colony of free love. Sometimes Frances called it a "school of love," and said it was to be established in the Pocono's. At other times she claimed it would be built in the heart of New York City. But always, it was Carl who was to act as Dilley's "chief aid in the work." At times Frances heard Minnie Dilley's voice itself "coming through the air" and telling her these things.

"They were nothing more than the wild imaginings of my insanely jealous wife's mind!" Carl suddenly cried. "The very idea is absurd. Miss Dilley never even intimated such a thing to me."

The three detectives gazed at the distraught man for a moment, before Sergeant Anning said sympathetically, "So in other words, Minnie Dilley was simply your landlord? You and your wife had no other relationship with her, right? And for some reason your wife developed this notion that Miss Dilley was trying to steal you away from her and…what?" He seemed to grope for the right word, "Make you king of some type of harem?"

Carl Thomsen, who had defended Minnie Dilley earlier, now backpedaled just a bit. Well, he began slowly, not exactly. While it was true that Frances believed Miss Dilley was trying to steal him away, he hinted that Minnie Dilley was not completely innocent in his wife's deterioration. The two women had had a "strange friendship," he said, and would spend many nights together reading "erotic literature." Carl claimed he was not happy with this arrangement, and often his wife would bring home these "erotic books" that Minnie Dilley would give her. Whenever he found such trash around the house, he would "throw the books in the ash can." It was for this reason that he decided to move his family away from Forty Fort, he said, "To free my wife from Miss Dilley's influence on her. My wife's life has been rendered miserable from her fear that we might be drawn into this cult against our will."

The longer they talked, the more bizarre the story became. It seemed clear that this meek little lumber salesman had some pretty peculiar beliefs of his own. Apparently, while Frances was certain that Minnie was exerting a strange influence over Carl, Carl believed Minnie was doing the same to his wife!

"Mr. Thomsen," Coughlin now asked, "what, exactly, was your relationship with Minnie Dilley?"

Carl sighed and leaned back in his chair. "My only relationship with Miss Dilley was that of a neighbor," he insisted. "In fact, I have not seen or talked to her since I left Forty Fort four years ago. I had no interest in her or her life."

"Do you think your wife could be responsible for Miss Dilley's murder?" Sergeant Anning suddenly asked.

Initially, Carl looked horrified by the suggestion, but when he answered, it was not a denial. "I don't know," he said softly, "I just don't know." He fell silent for a moment, his eyes dropping down to stare at the table top. Then, softly, almost in a whisper, he said, "She was gone from Wednesday to Saturday of that week, and I don't know where she went."

Anning glanced at Coughlin and Dempsey, feeling the same spark of excitement he now saw glinting in their eyes.

"What do you mean she was gone? What week?" Anning anxiously asked the distressed man.

"The week of the murder," Carl answered, finally looking up at him. "From April 1st to April 4th. She just disappeared. She left the kids with a neighbor, and she was gone. I didn't hear from her at all during that time, and when she returned on Saturday afternoon she refused to tell me where she had been."

"Did you report her absence to the police?" Dempsey asked.

Carl shook his head, admitting that he had not, and then said quietly, "It wasn't that unusual—not an uncommon occurrence. It had happened before."

~*~*~

On April 9, 1931 the three Luzerne County investigators, Coughlin, Dempsey and Anning, picked up Frances Thomsen and brought her to the Pittsburgh Police Station for questioning. At the same time, several Allegheny County detectives remained behind to complete a search of the Thomsen's home.

Frances appeared shy, quiet and timid initially, but once the questioning began, she maintained an attitude of calm indignation that police were treating her as a suspect in a brutal crime.

She had no problem with Minnie Dilley, she insisted. The two of them were close friends, and had always been on good terms. She knew nothing about her former landlord's murder, and certainly hadn't had anything to do with it.

"Mrs. Thomsen," A.D.A. Coughlin suddenly said, "Your husband tells us you were absent from home between April 1st and the 4th. Where were you over that period of time?"

"Oh that," Frances said, dismissing it, "that was nothing."

"Well," Coughlin said, "that may be Mrs. Thomsen, but we still need to know where you were."

"If you must know," Frances sniffed, "I was in the city looking for work."

Coughlin nodded. "I see. And where were you looking for work over those four days?"

Frances shrugged. "All over. I was all over the city, taking trains here and there, spending a lot of time in railway stations."

"Well, where were you specifically on that Friday, April 3, 1931?" It had been determined at autopsy that Minnie Dilley had been dead for at least 36 hours before her body was found, placing the time of death at Friday morning, April 3rd.

"Friday," Frances said, as if having to think about it. "Let's see, where was I on Friday? Oh, I remember now. I was in the employment agency at McCrory's, [a large department store in downtown Pittsburgh] looking for work."

"Okay," Coughlin continued, "so you were at McCrory's on Friday. Where were you on Thursday?"

Frances seemed to think for a moment, and then shrugged her shoulders. "I don't remember," she said.

"Well what else did you do on Friday, then? I mean, you weren't at McCrory's all day. Where else were you?"

"Just around the city looking for work," Frances answered.

Coughlin nodded. "I understand that, but could you be more specific? Where were you looking for work? Who did you see? Who did you talk to? Is there anyone who can verify your story for us?"

Frances simply shook her head. "No," she answered, "I can't remember anyone I saw during those four days, or anyone I talked to. I can't quite recall where all I made applications for work. I just don't know."

Coughlin sighed, "Well, where did you stay those four nights?"

Frances seemed to ponder the question for a moment, and then shook her head. "I'm not sure," she said, smiling. "I can't remember."

The three men looked exasperated. "Mrs. Thomsen," Coughlin suddenly said sternly, "You were gone for four nights. You had to have slept somewhere. Are you honestly telling us that you don't remember where you slept? Do you honestly think I believe that?"

"But it's true!" Frances cried, "I was in a lot of railway stations over those days."

"Did you sleep in the railway station?"

Frances looked amused. "Of course not," she said. "I was looking for work in the city."

"Did you apply for work at the railway station?" Dempsey asked, trying to make sense of her answers.

Frances laughed. "A woman applying for work at a railway station?" She seemed to find the question ridiculous. "Of course not. Elvira told me to look for work in the city."

Coughlin sat up straighter. "Elvira? Who is Elvira?"

"My daughter," Frances replied.

"How old is your daughter?" Coughlin asked.

"She'll be two this fall."

"And she told you to look for work in the city?" Coughlin's tone was incredulous.

"Yes," Frances answered. "I had to save our family."

"Save your family from what?" Dempsey asked.

"Elvira knows," The woman said, a knowing smile on her face.

Frances Thomsen would go on to give one incoherent answer after another throughout the long interrogation, making it clear to those interviewing her that the woman did, indeed, have some serious mental issues. None of the investigators believed Frances Thomsen was faking it. She had problems; there was no doubt about it. But they had been instructed not to probe too deeply with her. That was a job the Luzerne County District Attorney was looking forward to undertaking himself. As the three men brought the interview to a close, Frances suddenly asked if she could go home. Her request was denied, however, when Coughlin told her she would have to remain in the Pittsburgh jail pending verification of her alibi.

~*~*~

Despite the fact that the three investigators from Wilkes-Barre believed Frances Thomsen to be mentally deranged, they were still convinced she had brutally murdered Minnie Dilley, and they wanted to see her pay for that crime. They had orders to bring Frances back to Wilkes-Barre as soon as possible, where District Attorney Thomas Lewis intended to confront her with the threatening letters she had written to Minnie Dilley.

As Coughlin and the other investigators left the Pittsburgh Police Station, they were besieged by reporters who seemed increasingly angry that the police were vilifying a young mother. Why were they doing this, reporters shouted. What kind of evidence did they have that led them to believe this demure school teacher had anything to do with such a brutal crime?

The three men ignored the questions, until someone shouted out that they were wasting their time on a wild goose chase. At that, Coughlin stopped dead in his tracks and turned back to face the angry mob. "We are not on any wild goose chase," he said coldly. "As soon as we check the woman's statement we're going to rush right back to Wilkes-Barre with her."

The press seemed surprised by this admission and quickly called out more questions, but Coughlin and the others had already turned around and were rapidly walking away.

By later that evening, police had discovered that Frances' alibi of applying for work at McCrory's didn't check out. No one remembered interviewing her at the store, nor did she leave her contact information, which was not only customary but required.

Allegheny detectives had also reported that their search of the Thomsen house had produced several glass bottles of ginger ale identical in size and brand to that used to bludgeon Minnie Dilley.

That was enough for A.D.A. Coughlin, who immediately arrested the twenty-nine-year-old former schoolteacher on a charge of first-degree murder. He then made arrangements to have her transported back to Wilkes-Barre the next day.

~*~*~

Early on the morning of April 10, 1931, A.D.A. Coughlin, Sergeant Anning, and county detective Dempsey, along with their prisoner, began the 300 mile drive back to Wilkes-Barre from Pittsburgh. Upon arriving, the three lawmen took Frances directly to the Luzerne County courthouse where three additional men were waiting; Luzerne County District Attorney Thomas Lewis, Captain of the Pennsylvania State Police Wyoming Barracks William Clark, and Chief County Detective Richard Powell.

Frances continued to maintain her cool, calm composure, surprising this new round of interrogators as she had the last. Again, she denied everything; telling the men that she was on good terms with Minnie Dilley, and had nothing to do with her death. And Frances Thomsen would not budge, despite a grueling interrogation. It didn't matter if the people at McCrory's didn't remember her being there, she said; she had been there. It didn't matter if she couldn't remember where she had stayed for those three specific nights; it had been somewhere in Pittsburgh, not in Forty Fort. She had not been back to this part of the state in years, and she certainly had not killed Minnie Dilley.

Finally, after District Attorney Lewis had had enough, he confronted Frances Thomsen with the stack of letters she had written to the murdered spinster. Incredibly, Frances looked at the bundle of correspondence without batting an eye. Yes, she coolly admitted, she had written the letters. She had to, she said, in order to save her family. She and Minnie Dilley were in a fierce battle for the affections of Frances' husband, Carl.

"Miss Dilley wanted Carl to become the head of a love cult she was forming that would be made up of former teachers," Frances explained. That was why she was out looking for work during the time Minnie was killed, she said, because, "She offered my husband the lure of money, and I thought, well, if money is what he wants then I'll try to get a job to produce money."

District Attorney Lewis got right to the point. "Mrs. Thomsen," he said quietly, "I think you traveled to Forty Fort on April the first, and I think you went to Minnie Dilley's home, and I think while you were there, you bludgeoned her to death with a full bottle of ginger ale, and after that, you slit her throat."

"I did no such thing," Frances said calmly.

Those sitting with the prisoner seemed dumbstruck by her casual attitude. Despite her meek and mild appearance, Frances Thomsen was neither scared nor intimidated. In fact, the woman was as hard as nails. No one commented. Instead, the men simply sat there, staring at their prisoner. One minute ticked by; two minutes; three, four, five, and still, no one said a word.

Finally, Frances began to fidget. She glanced from the table to her interrogators and then back to the table again. She wrung her hands, then clasped them tightly in her lap, and soon, a thin crack began to appear on the surface of her tough veneer.

"I had no trouble with Miss Dilley," she said, looking directly at the three men. She glanced away when they still said nothing, and then, as if just remembering something, she reached for the stack of letters resting on the table.

"Look. Look here," she said, "If you look at these letters, you'll see that Miss Dilley and I were on good terms. Look at the last letter I wrote to her." She was leafing through the stack now, trying to locate the letter she was talking about.

Strange as it sounded, the three men knew that Frances was telling the truth. They had seen that, intermingled with all her threats and rantings about Minnie Dilley and her love cult, there were also sprinklings of praise and affection for the older woman. Frances had begged Minnie to allow her to come live with her and had written heartfelt pleas for Minnie to protect her. The very last letter Frances had written was sweet enough to give someone a toothache, but District Attorney Lewis believed this last letter was nothing more than a ploy on Frances' part; a way to gain entrance to the Dilley mansion. It had been written only four days before Minnie's body was found, making it highly likely that the old woman had received it just before she was killed.

The silence in the room seemed to rattle Frances, who abruptly threw the letters aside and covered her face with her hands. For the first time since the interview began, the suspected killer of Minnie Dilley appeared nervous. Suddenly, she turned to A.D.A. Coughlin and blurted, "If they put me in the electric chair, it will certainly be a joke."

Caught off guard by the comment, Coughlin seemed confused. "I don't understand," he began, but Frances Thomsen immediately interrupted him.

"Perhaps, I should say rather, it would be a travesty."

District Attorney Lewis stared at the young mother sitting across from him. He had been contemplating an action since the moment Frances had been returned to Wilkes-Barre and had decided that now was the right time to put it into play. He would take Frances Thomsen out to the mansion on River Street and confront her with the crime scene. Perhaps it would spook her enough to let down her guard. At least Lewis hoped so. He knew it would be the last chance he had to crack his suspect.

~*~*~

Members of the press had been loitering around the courthouse all day, well aware that the alleged slayer of Minnie Dilley was inside being interviewed by District Attorney Lewis. They were hoping for a chance to snap a picture of the accused killer, or at the very least, get a statement from the D.A., but it had been hours, and they were quickly getting restless. Around 3:00 in the afternoon, the mob of reporters saw a State Police car come from around the back of the courthouse, followed closely by a black sedan. When District Attorney Lewis was spotted in one of the vehicles, the press made a mad scramble to follow the entourage.

Soon, there was a line of automobiles winding their way the five miles from Wilkes-Barre to Forty Fort. Those living on River Street, noticing the parade of cars which pulled up in front of the Dilley mansion, quickly donned coats and shoes and rushed outside to see what was happening.

Frances appeared frightened by the crowd which was forming, and she clung to Donald Coughlin as the rest of his group quickly surrounded her and ushered her inside. Once in the mansion, those from the courthouse were met by Forty Fort Chief A.J. Klinger and Patrolman Sutliff.

Frances stiffened upon entering the house, and they could hear her breath catch in her throat. There before her, barely fifty feet away, lay Minnie Dilley's parlor, its massive stone fireplace staring at her like a sentinel guarding the secrets of the room. The sight of it stopped her dead in her tracks, and for a moment, she felt paralyzed.

The men were already entering the room, but Frances barely noticed them. She remained behind, unable to pull her gaze from the fireplace and the statue that rested on its mantle, gazing down upon her with unseeing eyes. Captain Clark, noticing his prisoner's reluctance, soon made his way back to her and lightly touched her shoulder. Gently, he began to coax her forward, leading her towards the room but just outside the entry, Frances halted again.

Clark watched as the color drained from her face, and her body began to tremble. She was shaking her head in a panic, attempting to break free of his grasp and back away. He noticed her eyes roll white in her head and then level back on him, and he saw that they were clouded with fear. For a moment, he thought she might faint and he instinctively tightened his grip on her arm.

Frances Thomsen did not faint, however. Instead, she began to moan, before suddenly blurting out, "Okay, okay, I did it! I did it! I had to do it, I had to. It couldn't be avoided."

For District Attorney Lewis, who stood watching from just inside the living room, Frances's words were like music to his ears, and he immediately felt a weight being lifted off his shoulders. No one spoke for a moment, and then Lewis moved towards Frances, gently taking her by the hands and guiding her into the room.

"It's okay," he said soothingly, leading her towards the settee. "It's okay. Everything is going to be okay."

Frances allowed him to lead her, and once in front of Minnie Dilley's sofa, the distraught woman sank wearily into it. Lewis sat next to her, continuing to hold her hand, comforting her.

"Frances," he finally said, "tell us what happened."

And after a shuddering sigh, Frances Thomsen did.

~*~*~

The story Frances told regarding the gruesome murder of Minnie Dilley was so bizarre, so fantastic, that it would leave all those who heard it dumbstruck. It contained all the elements needed to guarantee it a place in local legend and history, and the newspapers of the time had a field day with it. It was often compared to the 1928 hex murder of Nelson Rehmeyer, and for good reason; Frances Thomsen, like the three killers in the Rehmeyer case, also believed her victim was a witch.

As she sat on the sofa next to District Attorney Lewis, Frances began her story by saying that Minnie Dilley was, indeed, a witch who practiced witchcraft, and used her evil magic to "cast a spell over my husband."

Urging the wan killer to tell them what had happened, the eight men waited anxiously to hear her story. And Frances Thomsen did not disappoint.

Minnie Dilley, she said, had "mystic powers," and, "held a strange sway over me which she used to win the love of my husband from me." Although Frances claimed she had known about Minnie's "powers" for years, she said she had been unable to do anything about them. However, "when Miss Dilley decided to form a love cult and needed my husband to head it, I knew that I had to free him and myself from the sinister psychic control of her."

"Is that why you came here?" District Attorney Lewis asked, "Because you believed if Miss Dilley were dead, it would end her control over you and your husband?"

Frances, however, shook her head and insisted she had not come to kill the aged spinster. "I came here to make up with Miss Dilley after a quarrel we had two years ago. I came here with friendship in my heart, but she would have none of it."

Confused, Lewis smiled at the woman and said, "Why don't you start at the beginning. What happened on April 1st?"

Frances nodded. "Okay," she said, "April 1st. Well, as I said, I needed to free both me and Carl from Miss Dilley's mental persecution. I knew I could wait no longer, that the love cult was already in the works. So that Wednesday, I decided to take my children over to Mrs. Doots' apartment and see if she would watch them for me. She agreed, and I went back home, put a bottle of ginger ale in a bag, and hid a bread knife from my kitchen in the folds of my umbrella. After that, I started out for Forty Fort."

"How did you get here?" Lewis asked. "Did you drive or take the train?"

"No," Frances said, shaking her head, "I don't drive, and I had no money for the train. I hitchhiked here. I had no trouble getting rides, although there were a few times I had to walk a distance."

Those in the room were surprised by this revelation. It seemed hard to believe that this woman, who looked so gentle and submissive, had hitchhiked 300 miles, by herself, to reach Forty Fort. And then, having done so, went on to commit one of the most barbaric murders the town had ever seen.

As the tale unfolded, however, hitchhiking was nothing compared to the other surprising details Frances would relate. The entire confession was incredible, and the woman who was telling it one of the strangest people her questioners had ever met. Minnie Dilley's killer proved to be an enigma. While retaining an air of culture and refinement—her speech perfect, her grammar impeccable—the story Frances related was weird, delusional, and utterly nonsensical. An account that left those listening deeply unsettled.

Frances said she arrived in Forty Fort on Thursday afternoon, and "went directly to Miss Dilley's home, but she would not let me in. From there, I traveled up to Wilkes-Barre and spent the night."

"Where did you stay in Wilkes-Barre?" D.A. Lewis quickly interjected.

"I don't recall offhand," Frances answered. "But I came back to Miss Dilley's on the morning of April 3rd—Good Friday—and this time she allowed me to enter. When I walked in, I told her right off that I wished to discuss this cult which was breaking up my home. I wanted to inform her that Carl must not become her high priest as planned."

Minnie had led her into the parlor—this very room they now sat in—and Frances had taken a seat on this very sofa, while Miss Dilley sat down in the chair near the fireplace. She pointed to Chief Klinger, indicating that the chair he now sat in was the same one Minnie had occupied.

Of course, Miss Dilley had denied she was forming a love cult, Frances continued, but the longer they talked, the more frightened Frances had become.

"I could sense, in greater degree than ever before," Frances said, "the mental power of this woman that had enslaved my husband and was reaching out for me. It was then I decided only physical force could free me from a living death."

Frances dropped her gaze to the floor and fell silent. The only sound in the cavernous house was the ticking of the grandfather clock, the same sound that had unnerved Minnie's nephew the night he discovered her body.

After several minutes, Captain Clark cleared his throat uncomfortably, interrupting the silence. Grabbing the opportunity, District Attorney Lewis quickly asked, "Is that when you killed her?"

Frances' eyes grew wide and she shook her head. "I didn't kill her. I did it in self-defense." She looked pleadingly at the men. "It was her life or mine. I came here to make friends, but Miss Dilley refused. We had a quarrel, and then she attacked me."

"Miss Dilley attacked *you*?" Lewis asked, unable to hide his surprise.

"Yes," Frances answered, nodding her head. "I did it in self-defense. It was a case of physical strength versus mental strength."

Suddenly her voice cracked, the first real sign of remorse she had shown.

"It was then that I rendered her unconscious with the ginger ale bottle," she said, hesitating briefly before continuing. "And to make sure, I did the rest."

"You cut her throat?" District Attorney Lewis asked softy.

"Yes," Frances said simply.

Appearing to regain her composure, she went on to explain that, "After I rendered her senseless I used the knife as an additional precaution. It was her life or mine. I was sorry when I did it and I have been sorry ever since."

"Where did you have the knife? Lewis asked.

Frances thought for a moment, and then said, "I took it from inside of my umbrella. I believe I had set the umbrella here on the settee." She patted the cushion next to her. Afterwards, "I wiped the knife on a shawl and placed the shawl on the back of a chair."

"This chair?" Chief Klinger asked, indicating the chair he was sitting in and the one Minnie had allegedly occupied that morning.

Frances nodded and then shifted her eyes to the floor in front of the chair, where a stain marred the carpet. Pointing to it, she said casually, "That's where Miss Dilley fell when I struck her with the ginger ale bottle."

Captain Clark asked quietly, "Why did you do it Frances? What caused you to first strike her with the bottle?"

Frances' face took on a desperate appearance as she cried out, "I had to do it! She was using her psychic influence to destroy my home and my family! She was using us for experiments in persecution! My husband had fallen prey to such evil magic, and I had to do something to save us!" The tiny woman was so upset that by the end of these exclamations she had risen halfway off the sofa.

District Attorney Lewis suddenly pulled a strand of red glass beads from his pocket. The beads had been found in Minnie's parlor, near the edge of the fireplace, when police initially searched the house after the murder. None of the aged spinster's relatives recognized them, but because Minnie owned hundreds of pieces of jewelry, no one could say for sure that they were not hers. Lewis held the beads out to Frances and asked if they belonged to her.

Frances looked surprised when she saw the necklace, and immediately reached for it, taking the beads gently in her hands. Slowly sinking back on the settee, she nodded her head. "Yes," she said softly. "They're mine. They were a gift from my husband."

With his prisoner calm once again, Lewis got back to the questioning. "Frances, what did you do after you killed Miss Dilley?"

Frances said she had gone into the kitchen where she washed the blood from her hands, as well as the knife. She then hid the knife back in the umbrella, left the house, and immediately hitchhiked back to Pittsburgh, arriving on Saturday afternoon.

She appeared relieved after making her confession, and confirmed this when she spoke about her feelings after the murder.

"Once the deed was done," she said, "I felt a great fear and dread was lifted from me, and for the first time in months, I slept soundly."

The pale former-teacher then dropped her head and began biting nervously at the edge of her thumb. She glanced up shyly at the men around her, and then cast her gaze back to the floor. She appeared to have a question, but was hesitant to ask.

"What is it Frances?" Lewis asked.

"I was just wondering," she began, "My three children in Pittsburgh, do you know how they are? I'd like to see them."

Lewis, not wanting her to get distracted on a different subject, assured her the children were fine, and then asked her how she became aware of the love cult Miss Dilley was forming.

"The voices told me," Frances said immediately. "They told me every day. All the time the voices were screaming in my head, urging me to do something. I could feel the psychic influence Miss Dilley was having over Carl, convincing him to become the high priest of the cult. I had to end it. I had to save my family!"

"That woman was destroying us!" She shouted, rising from the sofa, her voice increasing in intensity. "She was a witch who had stolen my husband's love and wanted to share it with other women in her cult!"

Suddenly Frances swung around and pointed to the statue that rested on the mantle of Minnie Dilley's fireplace. "There," she cried out, "You see it, you see it? There. That's proof of Miss Dilley's love cult and her desire to have my husband reign over it."

Surprised, the men glanced up at the mantle, each taking a step closer to get a better look at the object which had so upset their prisoner. It was a beautiful piece, an intricately carved statue of a male figure with wings. The investigators knew nothing about art, however, and so had no way of knowing what the statue represented; it was the mythological figure of Eros, The God of Love.

~*~*~

The crowd which had initially formed around Minnie Dilley's mansion had grown in size, terrifying Frances Thomsen who had no desire to go outside and face them. Captain Clark made a mad dash for his squad car where he retrieved a khaki hued robe and wrapped his prisoner in it like a mummy. The robe covered Frances from head to toe, and obscured her face as the group of men shrouded her for the walk outside.

Instantly, the throng of people swarmed around them, eager to get a glimpse of Minnie Dilley's killer, and calling out questions to the trembling woman. The lawmen pushed the crowd back, as they ushered their prisoner ever faster into the backseat of Captain Clark's auto. Frances sunk down in the cushions, seeming to hope they would just swallow her up, as Trooper Annich hurriedly drove away.

District Attorney Thomas Lewis and A.D.A. Donald Coughlin stayed at the house in order to give a statement to the waiting press. Lewis did not want to publicly announce that Frances had confessed, but he told those gathered that he was confident she had killed Minnie Dilley on Friday morning, April 3, 1931, between 8 and 9 am.

Coughlin, who looked glum and shaken, told the reporters, "Personally, I do not believe Mrs. Thomsen is mentally sound and responsible for her actions. She will be given a sanity test as soon as our courts can act."

Later that day, the press no longer needed confirmation from the authorities that Frances had confessed. They had managed to intercept a telegram from Luzerne County Detective Richard Powell to Allegheny County Chief Detective George Murran which read: *Mrs. Carl Thomsen made a full confession regarding her part in the Minnie Dilley murder at Forty Fort Pa April 3, 1931.* That night, the evening papers screamed out news of the confession in bold black type.

A.A. McGuire, a brilliant and competent lawyer, was appointed as Frances' defense attorney and immediately called a press conference to discuss the case. Facing the eager reporters, he told them in no uncertain terms that his client would plead insanity.

"This woman is undoubtedly insane," McGuire began. "It must be remembered there are many forms insanity may take. We hold this woman followed an irresistible impulse—that she could not help what she did. During her confession at the house she stated just that; that she could not help what she did. She suffered obsessions. We have information she was insanely jealous of her husband, of any woman who was kind to him or to whom he frequently talked. It went even farther than that though," McGuire continued, "We have been told she was jealous even of her husband's men friends."

By the next morning, McGuire would have help with the case when two other defense attorney's, John Dando of Wilkes-Barre, and Louise McBride of Pittsburgh, were also retained to represent the young school teacher and mother of three. Louise McBride was a curiosity, since female lawyers defending murderers was a rarity, but the most surprising detail concerning these two new additions was who had hired them. It was not, as some people believed, Frances' family, but members of the alumnae association from the exclusive Wellesley College.

Incredibly, people who had never even met Frances Thomsen—but who lived in western Pennsylvania and had attended the same school as she—were immediately interested in her plight and rushed to offer their aid and assistance.

~*~*~

Frances was arraigned before Judge W.S. McLean on April 11, 1931, and much to the displeasure of the press, District Attorney Thomas Lewis had a few announcements to make before court. First off, he said, he was prohibiting any photos of the accused from being taken, and he was also planning to ask that the proceedings be closed to the press and public to prevent anyone from entering the courthouse with a hidden camera.

Immediately, the press called "foul," and Judge McLean threw them a bone. He would allow the proceedings to be open, but would bar any cameras from the courtroom.

Seated between two of her three attorney's, Frances looked small and weak as a charge of first-degree murder was leveled against her. She glanced towards the gallery where her husband, Carl, sat, looking frightened and distressed. Throughout the entire proceeding, Carl continuously glanced towards his wife, his look showing affection intermingled with bewilderment. He seemed unable to believe that he was sitting there, his wife standing before him charged with first-degree murder. Frances' parents, also present in the courtroom, knew exactly how he felt.

Before court, Frances had met with her family in the privacy of District Attorney Lewis' office, where the four of them shared a tear-filled reunion with hugs and kisses. Frances had seemed in good spirits then, although now she appeared morose and glum—though still calm and aloof—as McGuire and Dando entered a plea of not guilty for her.

Lewis called more than a dozen witnesses to take the stand at Frances' arraignment, including county detectives and state police, to testify about her arrest and the letters she had written to Minnie Dilley. Although Lewis introduced the letters into evidence, he declined to read them, another action that infuriated the press.

The most anticipated—and by far the most interesting—testimony came when Frances herself took the stand. The former school teacher appeared poised and confident, as she primly clasped her hands in her lap and sat up straighter in the hard wooden chair.

When Dando began by asking his client about the love cult, Frances glanced around the courtroom suspiciously, dropping her voice to a mere whisper.

"I am in great danger, I suppose, by saying," she began, obviously frightened, "because it includes a great many people in Forty Fort. But as far as I know, it is a plan to have a love cult, with my husband as the presiding man, for the purpose of health. Supposedly it is for women who are teaching or for other business reasons cannot have husbands. Minnie's final ambition was to build a sanitarium—a center she called "our little boarding place"—out in the mountains somewhere."

She hesitated for a moment, again glancing suspiciously around the courtroom, as if fearing there might be members of the "love cult" right there, ready to pounce upon her.

"They are still looking for a site to have it established," she continued, "by him, out there, to stay overnight."

This last sentence made no sense, and if those in the courtroom thought Frances had misspoken, they were wrong. The majority of her testimony was nonsensical, and her attorney, John Dando, did not have his client clarify anything she said. Nor did he have her elaborate on any of her testimony. Dando intended to let the judge and everyone else see how truly insane she was.

"I think it would take years for her to do it," Frances now said. "I don't think it would ever have materialized. That was her dream and she has had him on this course, in various cities we have been in, and I did not object. It is a modern idea, and all I have asked is not to be put out of the way, because I wanted to further our family life. And there I have been balked. She refused to let him take me out socially from the time we went to Homestead."

Frances' voice was beginning to rise, and she began to sound angry as she said, "Little by little she tried to have him put me off in the country as insane, and I refused to go because I'm not insane!" She paused, and then added, "Unless the recent act is insanity, and I am not sure about that. I know it was a terrible thing to do, but I have my reasons for it, and since we have been to Pittsburgh I tried to get work."

When Dando asked her about the actual murder itself, Frances shocked the entire courtroom when she said, "I deliberately severed her throat just as you would a chicken if you were fixing it for dinner, because I didn't dare let her live; did not dare let her suffer. Either she or I were going. I don't think it can be proved it was entirely in self-defense. I suppose if there is any help it will be me pleading insanity, but I am not insane. I was merely fighting for my life."

After the arraignment, Carl Thomsen returned to Pittsburgh, flabbergasted by the words that had come from his wife's mouth, while Frances' parents remained in Wilkes-Barre to be close to their daughter. District Attorney Lewis, himself badly shaken by Frances' testimony, told the press that he would commission a sanity board to examine her if her own lawyers didn't.

"I truly believe Frances Thomsen is insane," Lewis said bluntly.

John Dando was pleased to hear the District Attorney's statement, and thrilled to have it on record. Dando was a smart and capable lawyer who had been in contact with one of the top criminal defense attorney's in the city of Boston, Ira Parquarhar. Parquarhar had pledged his assistance, even offering to travel to Wilkes-Barre, but Dando told him that wouldn't be necessary. Frances' attorney believed that Prosecutor Lewis had just helped his case and the plan he had been formulating for his client's defense.

Now, as he faced the press, Dando confirmed that Frances' defense would be a defense of insanity, but, he stressed, it would be a defense of "temporary" insanity only.

Going on to explain further, the attorney said, "Mrs. Thomsen was deranged when she killed Minnie Dilley, but the killing has removed the insanity, and now she is cured."

It was an incredible statement and a brilliant defense. If believed, there was an excellent chance that Frances Thomsen would walk out of prison a free woman—even if convicted of Minnie Dilley's murder—without ever being punished for her crime.

~*~*~

All those who listened to Frances Thomsen's story, or spent any time with her, honestly believed that she was mentally deranged. However, there were still a few things that nagged at some of the investigators' minds.

For instance, the last letter Frances wrote to Minnie Dilley was full of praise and affection, and appeared to have been written for the sole purpose of gaining entry to the spinster's home. Could a crazy person truly be so calculating and cunning?

There was also the jealousy Frances carried for her husband. Witnesses had said that when Carl Thomsen installed a radio for Minnie Dilley, Frances had gone ballistic at the fact that he was alone with her in her mansion. It didn't seem to matter to Frances that her landlord was 43 years older than her husband; she was insanely jealous regardless.

There were some who insisted that the 'love cult' story was pure make-believe on Frances' part. That, in fact, Frances hated Minnie not only because she was jealous of her, but because of an incident that had occurred when she and Carl were living across the street from her. At one point, annoyed that there were toys all over the yard, and the grass had not been mowed, Minnie had chastised Frances for being a poor housekeeper and a "misfit wife." The statement had allegedly infuriated Frances—so some said—and was the catalyst that ended the two women's friendship.

It was an interesting story. Could Frances have actually been faking her insanity, Thomas Lewis wondered? Although deep down he honestly didn't think she *had* faked it, Lewis had no intention of letting Francis get away with murder. Whether the woman was crazy or not, he had been appalled by the statement Dando made about temporary insanity.

Shortly thereafter, when District Attorney Lewis discovered what Frances' life was like down at the county jail, his anger only increased. Frances Thomsen was apparently the new "celebrity" at the prison, someone who considered herself very special, and above the other inmates incarcerated with her.

Lewis had no idea what the deal was with Wellesley College, but he was beginning to get mighty sick and tired of those who had once gone to school there. The day after her arraignment, Frances had been visited in her cell by four Wellesley alumni who brought with them baskets of delicacies for her. These included cheese, fruit and crackers, scores of reading material, and several perfumed toiletries, such as soap, powder, and lotion. The four women comforted the prisoner, and assured her that they, and others, would do all they could to help her.

Before leaving the jail, the Wellesley women met with Warden Healey and his jail officials, and told them they were there to help Frances, and would be visiting her regularly. They would prefer, however, if their help and their visits were kept secret, insinuating that it was in the prisoner's best interest if she, and they, were shielded from the press.

When Warden Healey told them he'd be happy to see what he could do, they then requested that Frances be provided with every comfort and luxury permitted by the jail—including special medical attention—assuring her jailer that they would foot the entire bill.

The reaction Frances' plight had unleashed in Wellesley College alumnae was astonishing. They were not only paying for two of her attorneys, but also having outside meals delivered to the jail, showering her with gifts, and covering the costs of all her medical needs.

Frances' troubles seemed to be a magnet which drew together former graduates of Wellesley like nothing else could. In fact, there had once been an organization, known as the Wellesley Alumnae Association of Northeastern Pennsylvania, which counted in its membership some of the most influential, talented, and socially prominent women in the state. Little by little, however, the organization had gradually died away, and they had not held a meeting in more than ten years, but the widespread attention Frances' arrest had produced had immediately changed that. Already there were plans to call a meeting of the organization in the next few days in order to arrange aid for their fallen classmate's defense.

Since the four women had come to visit, Frances was also receiving special privileges at the jail. Unlike her fellow inmates, she was excluded from doing any menial tasks around the facility, and after breakfast was allowed to relax in her cell until the noon meal was served. Afterwards, she would have her recreation period and then attend church each day from 3 to 4:00 pm. She spent all her free time in her cell, reading volumes of books sent to her by her former Wellesley graduates or borrowed from the jail library.

Even more disgusting to the prosecutor was the fact that since the visit from the Wellesley College alumni, Francis' spirits had lifted immeasurably. Now, not only was she showing great improvement in her health and general demeanor, but she was eating well, sleeping soundly, and her speech, once crammed with illogical incoherencies, was now completely rational.

The only thing people still found strange about Frances Thomsen was that she showed no interest in her three children who remained in Pittsburgh, being cared for by family and friends. She never asked about them, never inquired as to their welfare, and had no pictures of them adorning the walls of her cell.

~*~*~

Days passed and little was heard on the Dilley case. It was expected that John Dando would file for a sanity hearing on Frances immediately, but that was not the case. District Attorney Lewis had vowed to file for the hearing himself if Dando didn't, but all was quiet on his front as well. Finally, on April 18, 1931, Warden William Healey filed his own petition for a lunacy commission on Frances' sanity.

The Sanity Commission was comprised of Dr. Stanley Freeman and attorney Joseph Fleitz, both of Wilkes-Barre, and Dr. W.T. Baskett, superintendent of Retreat Mental Hospital in Newport Township.

In questioning Frances, the group asked if she believed she had been directed by God to kill Minnie Dilley, and Frances admitted that she didn't know.

"I don't know if I killed at a divine command," she said, adding, "but I thought it was right; that there was nothing else to be done."

Frances was asked to tell, in her own words, why she had killed Minnie, and Frances, tired of re-hashing the murder, sighed wearily before she did.

"Because she would not let me live with my family and because she was an evil spirit and I felt it was the one thing for me to do," she said. "I killed her in the name of God. I killed her in the name of the government of the United States; for family life and the moral welfare of little children."

She went on to say that "there was absolutely no doubt Miss Dilley wielded an unholy and evil influence over my husband. I needed to protect him and my home and our children from it."

Frances claimed she had been in "holy terror" of Minnie Dilley for a long time "because she had previously tried to take my life by not permitting me medical aid when my last baby was born. And also by trying to persuade my husband to use poison," here she dropped her voice and grinned mischievously, "but he never would because he loves me underneath it all...don't hurt my husband, because if it were not for him I would not have been warned."

Frances went on to say that after bludgeoning Minnie Dilley, and attempting "to cut her head off," she had gone "out to the street. I felt as if I had been underwater and needed to come up for air. I went to a window where there was a little baby and the baby smiled at me, and lingered at the window, *just five minutes after I had killed her*, so I don't feel as if I were bad. As if I did anything wrong."

On April 27, 1931, the sanity commission handed down their findings. According to them, Frances Thomsen was suffering from paranoia and "obsessions," beset by "delusions of persecution, grandiose ideas, and a fiendish belief of being wronged." It was their conclusion that she was, indeed, insane, and had probably been so for many years. It was also their opinion that her insanity was incurable.

The commission's findings meant that Frances would not be going to trial, but instead would be sent to Retreat Mental Hospital, in Newport Township, Luzerne County, for treatment. District Attorney Lewis, however, not forgetting those nagging doubts, moved to delay her trip to the hospital until he could take her case before the grand jury and ask for a murder indictment, as well as a detainer against her. With a detainer, should Frances Thomsen someday be judged cured and sane, the detainer would prevent her from being released. Instead, she would be returned to Luzerne County where she would have to stand trial for the first-degree murder of Minnie Dilley.

On May 5, 1931, Lewis got his wish. The Grand Jury not only handed down an indictment against Frances, but a detainer as well. Frances Thomsen, the college graduate and former school teacher, was quickly driven to Retreat Mental Hospital and admitted, supposedly to live out the remainder of her days. Whether she did or not, is unknown. Nothing else was ever heard of her.

Postscript:

Retreat Mental Hospital closed its door for good in 1980. Their admissions, releases, and death records have been restricted to access, making it impossible to determine whatever became of Frances Thomsen, her husband, or any of her children. There is no indication that she was ever tried for Minnie Dilley's murder.

Curiously, the Dilley case has been almost completely forgotten to history. Having lived in this area all my life, I had never heard of it. When I happened to come across a small newspaper article pertaining to it, I found it absolutely fascinating. When I then began researching it, and discovered how truly bizarre it actually was, I felt it was a story worthy of putting in a book for others who might be interested to learn of it.

THE KILLER OF COATESVILLE

(Coatesville, PA. The brutal murder of Helen Moyer.)

Sixteen-year-old Helen Moyer was in a hurry to get going as she gathered up her schoolbooks, waved goodbye to her classmates, and rushed out the door. Momentarily startled by the blast of icy wind that hit her square in the face, Helen grimaced at the thought of the walk that lay before her. Usually, the young girl enjoyed her walk home from school—it gave her a chance to think—but on this particular Thursday, February 11, 1937, she wasn't looking forward to it. It was the dead of winter in Southeastern Pennsylvania, bitterly cold, and Helen's walk was a long one.

A sophomore at the Coatesville High School, Helen lived with her parents and siblings in the small town of Modena, three miles away. The Moyers were a close knit family, deeply religious, well-liked, and highly respected in the area. Helen's parents, Absalom and Melba[1], were extremely proud of their children, all of whom were good kids who never gave them cause to worry.

Helen was the type of child every parent wishes for: pretty, popular, kind, generous, and never too busy to lend a helping hand. She loved her family, made friends easily, and had a way with both animals and children. Her teachers thought the world of her, not only because she was a good student who received excellent grades, but because she was always polite and courteous as well. She was active in her church—the Hepzibah Baptist Church in Coatesville—where she served as a Sunday school teacher and dreamed of one day becoming a missionary.

Helen Moyer was a responsible young lady, mature beyond her years, and everyone knew it. Which is why there was so much panic when she disappeared while walking home from school on that cold February day.

~*~*~

---

[1] Sometimes also referred to as Nellie.

Helen's mother waited for her that Thursday afternoon, peering through her living room window, hoping to see the familiar figure of her daughter hurrying down the street. She couldn't understand what was keeping the girl, and, for the past forty-five minutes, had been considering possible explanations for her absence. Had Helen stopped to talk to someone, she wondered, or been held after school for some reason? Melba thought it unlikely, and when she glanced at the clock and saw that it was nearly 5:00 pm, her worry turned to fear. Helen was already an hour late and it was beginning to get dark. Melba knew there could be no logical explanation for this tardiness; something was obviously wrong.

Stepping away from the window, the worried mother began to pace, wringing her hands nervously as she thought about the weather and the fact that Helen wasn't dressed for it. Her daughter had left home that morning in a flowered dress, a red knit sweater, and her brown coat with matching hat—fine attire for her brisk walk home in the daylight, but it was much colder now and almost dark.

Melba continued pacing until she saw the approaching headlights splash across the living room window. At that point, the panic that had been building finally erupted. *Thank God*, the terrified woman thought, breaking into sobs; *thank God*. Melba knew the headlights signaled the arrival of her husband home from work, and she hurried to the door and swung it open, waiting anxiously for Helen's father to appear.

~*~*~

Absalom Moyer had put in a long day at the Veteran's Hospital where he worked, and he was hoping for nothing more than a hot meal and a good night's sleep when he arrived home. But as he turned into his driveway and noticed his house lit up like a Christmas tree—and then his wife standing outside the front door waiting for him—he immediately sensed that his hopes were about to be dashed.

The sight of his wife—hysterical and rushing towards the car—sent a wave of terror crashing over him. Melba looked panic stricken as she ran blindly towards him, reaching out before collapsing into his outstretched arms.

"What's wrong?" Absalom demanded, scared now. "What happened?"

But his wife was unable to speak through her tears. Realizing this, Absalom, his heart beating wildly in his chest, began leading her towards the house, continuing to ask what was wrong.

It wasn't until they were just inside the front door that Melba Moyer finally found her voice, blurting out that Helen had never come home from school. Absalom felt his breath catch and his stomach lurch. He knew his daughter; she was one of the most reliable and responsible people he had ever met. If Helen hadn't come home from school, then something was drastically wrong.

Reluctant to let his wife see the terror her news had wrought—and Absalom Moyer had never experienced fear like he was feeling right then—he dropped into a chair to steady himself.

After taking a moment to regain his composure, Helen's father went directly to the phone and began calling friends and neighbors, enlisting the aid of anyone willing to help. Soon, a posse of men, dressed in warm clothing and armed with flashlights, were gathered at the Moyer house waiting for instructions from the missing girl's father.

Absalom suggested they begin by searching the three mile stretch of road between his house and Coatesville, and the others quickly agreed, readying themselves to go. Picking up his own flashlight, Absalom glanced at his wife and saw the same fear he was feeling radiating from her eyes. He was anxious to get going, but he hesitated for a moment, going to her and taking her gently in his arms.

"I'll find her," he said firmly, staring intently to emphasize his words.

Melba gave a forced smile and nodded. Then, desperately trying to control her ragged emotions, she let out a shuddering sigh and turned away. She didn't want her husband to see her crying again.

Absalom wanted to comfort her and reached for her again, then stopped. He realized there could be no comfort for this predicament until he found his daughter and brought her home. Quickly, he turned toward those gathered in his house.

"Okay, let's go," he said, opening the front door.

~*~*~

Retracing the route Helen would have walked, the group of searchers drove slowly along Modena Road towards Coatesville, pointing their flashlights out open windows and calling out the girl's name. With their car heaters blasting, they scanned the sides of the road and craned their necks to peer into ditches, realizing for the first time just how lonely and desolate that stretch of highway actually was. It was dark and eerie, consisting mainly of thick trees and woods only occasionally interrupted by open fields still bearing the remnants of the last fall harvest. There were no people to be seen, and no cars passed as the men drove steadily forward, searching for the missing girl.

About a mile into their journey, Absalom's headlights illuminated something on the opposite side of the road. He brought his car to a jolting halt and leapt out, his flashlight revealing a jumbled pile of paper and schoolbooks scattered along the berm. He picked up a piece of paper and felt a sense of dread descend upon him. He recognized the familiar script of his daughter's handwriting and realized that the books and papers were hers.

Within moments another searcher called from a few feet up the road. "Over here," the man yelled, waving his flashlight in the direction of something lying on the ground.

Rushing over, Absalom saw a woman's hat resting in the street, and only a few feet away, a pair of ladies shoes. He stared at them, his mind reeling, as he recognized Helen's belongings.

"Oh, my God," Absalom whispered. "Helen," he cried, swinging the beam of light towards the seemingly impenetrable woods. "Helen!"

All of the men followed suit and began calling out the missing girl's name but their voices held little enthusiasm. They didn't expect an answer, and each of them felt sick to his stomach. What had happened seemed obvious; Helen must have been hit by a car and was probably lying somewhere close-by, dead.

Absalom, however, intent on finding his daughter, scrambled down the roadway bank and began working his way into the woods. After only a few minutes, two of the searchers went after him, grasped him by the shoulders and attempted to guide him back to his car. Absalom tried to shrug the men off, but they held tight, urging him to go with them.

"We need to get help," one of them said softly. "More searchers, better flashlights, and the police—we need to call the police."

Those last words stopped Absalom in his tracks. He knew the men were right and, reluctantly, allowed himself to be led back to his car. *We need to get help*, Absalom kept telling himself. *We need to find Helen.*

~*~*~

It was just after 6:00 pm when the call came into the Coatesville Police Station and Captain Ralph Williams answered the phone. It took a few seconds for the officer to understand what the distraught caller was saying, but when he heard the words "never came home from school," and "Modena Road," the lawman sat up straighter in his chair. *Modena Road again,* Ralph Williams thought as he grabbed his coat and hurried from the station. Modena Road had figured prominently in several calls to the Coatesville Police lately, and the more the captain thought about it, the more anxious he was to get there and find out what had happened now.

When Captain Williams arrived at the scene, it took him barely a minute to feel a sinking sensation in the pit of his stomach. He had seen plenty of accidents in his day, and as he noted the tattered books and papers, and bent to examine the shoes, he was convinced that that was what he was looking at right now; an accident.

Helen's shoes were torn, in fact split wide open along the seams—a strange phenomenon, but one he had seen before. When a person was stuck by a car, the impact sometimes knocked the individual right out of their shoes. While the body might be flung hundreds of yards away, the victim's shoes were often left sitting side by side on the pavement, as if their owner had simply taken them off and left them there. And that's what Williams was seeing here; evidence that pointed to Helen Moyer having been the victim of a hit and run driver.

Like those who had originally begun searching for the missing girl, Williams believed that Helen's body was lying somewhere nearby, and he sure as hell didn't want the girl's father there when he found it. He didn't have to worry. One look at those pitch black woods surrounding the road convinced Williams that little would be found that night. It was simply too dark to do a thorough search; they would have to wait until morning.

After leaving his men with instructions to walk the road and search all the ditches, Williams headed back to the Coatesville Station to place a call to the Pennsylvania State Police. The small-town captain knew he would need help looking for Helen's body, as well as searching for the hit and run driver.

~*~*~

By dawn of the next day, Friday, February 12, 1937, local and state police—along with more than 100 volunteers—were scouring Modena Road and tramping through the woods in a desperate effort to find Helen Moyer's body. No one believed the girl would be found alive; if the accident hadn't killed her, the sub-zero temperatures from the night before would have.

About a hundred yards beyond her schoolbooks, investigators came across the lens from a broken automobile headlight, giving them further proof that Helen had been struck by a car. Although there was no blood visible on the lens, there *were* strands of blondish hair clinging to it that appeared to be the same color and length as Helen Moyers.

As the morning passed and the search expanded into ever widening terrain, law enforcement officials began to feel uneasy. *Where was Helen's body?* They should have found the girl by then, but there was no trace of her. They wondered how far a car could have thrown her, and decided fairly quickly that it couldn't have been *that* far.

Almost a mile from where Helen's books were discovered, searchers came upon a woman's bloodstained slip. Excited by the discovery, Corporeal C.M. Ross of the Pennsylvania State Police had it immediately taken to Melba Moyer for identification. Although Helen's mother studied the slip closely for several minutes, she eventually shook her head. She didn't recognize the undergarment, she said. It did not belong to her daughter.

A half mile beyond that discovery police found another: a torn silk scarf, and a section of a man's white shirt with the buttons torn off. Corporeal Ross had no idea if this find was significant or not, but he had his troopers gingerly slip the evidence into brown paper bags, and then seal and label them.

Despite the fact that more and more volunteers were showing up to help with the search, Ross's hopes of finding the girl were rapidly beginning to fade. He believed Helen *had* been hit by a car, but he was becoming convinced that the driver had panicked and either taken her body with him or hidden it somewhere to cover up the accident. There was really no other explanation. Local and state police had been conducting a grid-pattern search along the road and deep into the woods, and had covered nearly a mile without any results. Everyone knew that if Helen had been left where she landed after being struck, they would have found her by now.

County Detective Francis Grubb tended to agree. At most, he thought the body should have been within a few hundred yards of Helen's personal belongings, and wondered if the driver had taken the girl to get medical help. Calls to local hospitals in the area all proved negative, however. None had admitted or treated, an injured girl either the day or night before.

Mayor Albert R. Bergstrom was informed of Helen's disappearance and the inability of the police to find her body, and thought the whole thing sounded wildly bizarre. However, it wasn't until he was shown a picture of the missing girl that he felt the hair on the back of his neck stand on end. Bergstrom was a former police superintendent, and his mind still worked like a cop. He knew that only one week earlier another young girl, who looked similar enough to Helen Moyer to be her sister, had been attacked at virtually the same spot where Helen had disappeared.

The crime had occurred on February 4, 1937, as fifteen-year-old Jennie Watterson was walking home from the Coatesville School. At about 3:45 in the afternoon a green truck had pulled up alongside her and a young man offered her a ride. It was freezing out that day, and although apprehensive about it, Jennie accepted the man's offer and climbed into his truck. Everything seemed fine as the two rode along until just before they reached Modena. At that point, the man suddenly grabbed a screwdriver that was resting on the seat between them and hit Jennie with it. The girl, shocked and afraid, let out a scream, but the man simply continued to drive as if nothing had happened.

There was a bend in the road (where Helen's belongings would be found a week later) and as the man slowed his truck to ease into this same turn, Jennie Watterson threw open her door and tumbled out of the vehicle. The girl hit the pavement, then got to her feet and ran.

Surprised, the man screeched to a halt and chased after her, still brandishing the screwdriver. At the edge of the woods he caught her and grabbed hold, but Jennie, afraid and fighting, managed to break free of his grasp and bolt into the woods. She ran blindly, crashing through briars and brambles, afraid to pause even for a moment. Luckily, the terrified girl was successful in eluding her attacker, and other than some scratches and bruising, was not seriously injured in the attack.

The frightened teen described the man as "about twenty-years-old, with dark hair, a husky build, and a neat appearance." He had been wearing overalls, Jennie said, and she assumed he was a mill hand coming home from work, but she had no idea who he was.

Now, as Bergstrom studied the picture of Helen Moyer, he realized that not only did she and Jennie resemble each other, but they each wore the same color coat and hat. Could Helen have been a case of mistaken identity? Tapping the photo on the edge of his desk, Bergstrom thought it highly possible. Jennie Watterson's attacker could have lain in wait on that isolated road, hoping to see Jennie again so he could run her down and eliminate the only witness to his attack. He could have easily mistaken Helen for her since the two girls looked so much alike, and wore the same color coat and hat. That would also explain why police hadn't found Helen's body. On discovering his mistake, the attacker could have taken the girl away to try and hide his crime.

The more Bergstrom thought about it, the more convinced he became that this was exactly what had happened. In fact, the Mayor was so sure about his theory, he didn't even bother to wait for detectives to investigate further. The next day, February 13, 1937, he related his hypothesis to the eagerly waiting press.

"There is no doubt in my mind," Bergstrom said with conviction, "that this girl was killed and her body spirited away by her murderer. Helen was killed intentionally, in a case of mistaken identity."

Bergstrom's words, and his theory, both startled and shocked the community. This was the first indication that whatever had happened to Helen Moyer may not have been an accident. In some respect, most people could see—if not understand—how a driver, "freaking out" after just having hit someone, might be so distressed and fearful that they took the body away in a panic. Few, however, had considered the possibility that Helen might have been intentionally run down and murdered. The very thought caused an uproar throughout the area, and sent even more people scrambling to try and find her.

By that same afternoon, more than 500 men and boys—including the entire local Boy Scout Troop—had rallied together to search ditches, woods, abandoned properties, and waterways. They dragged nearby Brandywine Creek, and drained a pond in the small town of Montoursville a few miles away. While Helen's family was grateful for their help and effort, the throng of volunteers worried the authorities. Several of the men were openly brandishing firearms and threatening to dispense their own justice should Helen's killer be found. Fearing the mob might become violent, police tried to assure them that there was no evidence that the missing girl had been murdered. It did little good, however; Mayor Bergstrom's announcement had unleashed a fury, and it appeared the residents of Coatesville and Modena were out for blood.

~*~*~

By February 14, Valentine's Day, Helen had been missing for three days, and still no one could say what had actually happened to her. Worst yet, even those in authority couldn't agree on a theory for the pretty sixteen-year-old's disappearance.

Mayor Bergstrom and Chief Ralph Williams believed the girl had been killed in a case of mistaken identity. Williams had investigated the Jennie Watterson case, and he felt the similarities between her attack and Helen's disappearance were more than a coincidence. The Pennsylvania State Police and County Detective Francis Grubb, however, felt that Helen had been hit accidentally and the driver had taken her body in a panic. And now, the former chief of the Coatesville Police, Burgess Carl Jeffries, decided to chime in with his own opinion.

Jeffries called a press conference to announce that several Modena civic leaders were offering a $500 reward in the Moyer case, and it was his intention to ask the Chester County Commissioners to match that sum as well. "Part of this $1000 will probably be paid for information leading to the girl's body if she is dead," Jeffries said, "but, I am satisfied the girl is alive, and more and more people are thinking the same way."

Surprised, the gathered reporters waited for an explanation.

"We have searched the surrounding countryside thoroughly," Jeffries said, "and while it is possible we might have missed a slight nook, I am satisfied the girl is alive, *and was never hit by an automobile in the first place.*"

Appearing dumbstruck for a moment, no one spoke. For four days authorities had claimed that Helen had been struck by a car, either accidentally or on purpose, and now the former chief was espousing a brand new suggestion—and, as they soon found out, an astonishing one at that.

Jeffries believed that Helen had been "taken by a white slave ring who kidnapped her to be used for immoral purposes." Not only that, however, but also "that any evidence of her being struck by a car—her shoes, hat, and books in the road—were left there purposely to make it look like an accident and throw police off the trail."

Most people scoffed at Jeffries notion, but they might have been surprised to find out that several investigators also believed the "accident" could have been staged. One of the most often discussed scenarios among authorities was that Helen had simply run away and staged the scene herself.

The many theories being thrown out as to what might have happened to Helen greatly upset her family and friends. The residents of Modena, feeling that the case was being badly bungled by local officials, decided to get together and send a telegram to J. Edgar Hoover of the FBI. "All signs point towards a kidnapping," the telegram read, "and we are begging you to enter the case."

The FBI declined to become involved, however, informing the residents of Helen's hometown that "there is no evidence the girl has been taken over state lines."

Crushed by their refusal, Helen's father personally sent President Franklin D. Roosevelt a telegram pleading with him "as one father to another," to assign Federal Agents to the case. "Local police have done everything possible," Absalom wrote, "but we need trained investigators to find my daughter."

Roosevelt, too, refused to interfere with the case, leaving the job of finding Helen to local and state police.

~*~*~

The same day Burgess Jeffries spoke to the press, police finally got their first break in the Moyer case.

That afternoon, fifty-five-year-old William Crawford, an African American scrap worker from the town of Modena, appeared at the Coatesville Police Department to relate something he had seen on the afternoon of February 11. Crawford told the police that on that particular Thursday he had been driving a horse and wagon along Modena Road at about the same time Helen had disappeared. Like Helen, Crawford had been traveling south, from Coatesville to Modena, and was about 300 yards from where Helen's books were found, when suddenly a green truck sped past him and swerved for no apparent reason. When the truck swerved, Crawford continued, he had seen what he thought was "a flock of white pigeons whirling up from the ground."

The truck had continued on for a moment, before skidding to a halt and backing up. While doing a U-turn in the road, the driver had scraped the side of his truck along a telephone pole, before vanishing from Crawford's sight around the bend in the road. Within minutes, however, the truck had reappeared again and sped past Crawford in the opposite direction from which it had come, this time going towards Coatesville.

Excited by his story, Captain Williams asked the man if he happened to get the plate number on the truck, but Crawford shook his head, indicating that he had not. Nor had he noticed Helen's shoes, books, or hat in the road. But he had gotten a good look at the truck, which he described as being fairly new, green in color, and carrying what appeared to be beer kegs in the back.

An examination of the telephone pole showed three marks on it, one of them still bearing fresh flakes of green paint. Captain Williams was convinced that Crawford had been an eyewitness to Helen Moyer's hit and run. He theorized that what the scrap worker thought was a flock of white pigeons whirling up from the ground was actually Helen's schoolbooks and papers being flung into the air as she was struck.

When Captain Williams received test results indicating the broken headlamp was from a 1935 or newer vehicle, he breathed a sigh of relief. That corroborated Crawford's assessment of the truck being fairly new. Finally, the police captain thought, a place to start.

~*~*~

On February 15, authorities descended on the towns of Modena and Coatesville, stopping any green truck they saw and interviewing its owner. They checked parking lots and driveways, spoke to area residents, and made a list of people who might own such a vehicle. One of the names the officers heard repeated quite often was that of John Ward*, a Modena farmer.

Ward was twenty-three-years-old and had never been in any type of trouble with the law, but when police tried to track the young man down, they couldn't find him. Wondering if he had fled, authorities began searching for him.

Meanwhile, Detective Francis Grubb was on his way to investigate *another* incident occurring on Modena Road that same afternoon. Someone had tried to lure another young female into his truck.

When Grubb arrived at the girl's house, he was met by her upset mother who led him into the kitchen where her young daughter waited. The detective was stunned to see that the victim was little more than a toddler, just six-years-old, and obviously frightened. Grubb listened as the child told him about a man who had stopped her on Modena Road and tried to get her to go for a ride in his green truck. Once again, her description of the driver matched that of Jennie Watterson's attacker nearly two weeks earlier.

Detective Grubb didn't mind admitting that he was scared to death when he left the little girl's house. What kind of monster was roaming the road between Modena and Coatesville, he wondered? It was one thing to kidnap a pretty teenage girl, whose physique was that of an adult, but it was something else entirely to attempt to abduct a six-year-old child. It was an altogether different crime, perpetrated by an altogether different kind of criminal. Grubb knew that whoever the man in the green truck was, he needed to be caught immediately.

Late that same evening, John Ward, having heard that police were looking for him, voluntarily turned himself in to State Police. Ward was taken to an interrogation room while other state troopers went out to the parking lot to take a look at his truck. Interestingly, they noted that Ward's truck was not only green in color, but it had a broken headlamp as well. Peering into the cab, the officers felt even more excited to see several long strands of light colored hair that looked similar to that found on the broken headlight at the scene of Helen's disappearance.

Ward's questioning had been routine up that point, but when his interrogators learned what was discovered in and around his truck, their demeanor immediately changed. No longer amiable with their suspect, the officers badgered the young man, and openly accused him of murdering Helen Moyer and spiriting her body away. Ward adamantly denied knowing anything about the girl's disappearance or hitting her with his truck. His headlight had been broken when he hit a deer, he said, and he insisted he had been nowhere near Modena Road on February 11.

Police collected the hair from Ward's truck and rushed it to Philadelphia for testing, and then locked the young man up pending the results. Although Ward seemed like a good suspect, authorities were disappointed to see that beyond the broken headlight, there was no other damage to his truck. No scrape down either side and no dents or scratches anywhere else.

Soon, chemical analysis also revealed that the hair found in Ward's truck was not Helen Moyer's, and when Jennie Watterson failed to identify him as her attacker, police had no choice but to let the young man go.

~*~*~

On February 17 officers began interviewing Helen's female classmates to establish if any of them had encountered a man who tried to lure them into a vehicle. Incredibly, one young girl they spoke to said that she, too, had been stopped by a man in a green truck who offered both her and her little brother a ride. The incident had occurred around the end of January, but definitely before Jennie Watterson was attacked. The man had tried to coax the two into his truck, but had not been persistent when the girl said no.

So far, authorities had a man in a green truck attempting to lure two girls into his vehicle, attacking another, and possibly running down Helen Moyer. Those were the known victims, but were there more? And was the same man responsible for each of the incidents? If it *was* the same man, police were baffled as to what type of individual they were dealing with. Never before had they encountered such a predator. Even more alarming was the fact that the most recent attempted abduction—the six-year-old girl—had occurred four days *after* Helen disappeared. If it was the same man who was responsible for all of them, then Helen's death hadn't appeased him. Her murder had apparently only intensified whatever sinister and lustful desires the man possessed. Whoever he was, authorities knew one thing for certain; they needed to find him and find him fast.

Area residents were just as eager to have the man in the green truck caught, and they continued to flood the police with tips—often more than a hundred a day. Most turned out to be useless, but some excited the investigators and gave them hope, like the one that came in shortly after John Ward was released.

It was early evening when an obviously nervous man called the State Police barracks to report that his son had just discovered a recently dug grave. The boy and a friend had been hiking through the woods about a mile outside of Coatesville, when the two had come upon the secret burial site and rushed home to summon help.

Although it was already dark out, troopers responded to the call immediately and, using flashlights, had the boys lead them back to the site. The longer they walked through the woods, however, the more discouraged the officers became. They were being led far away from any road or highway, and it didn't seem plausible that *anyone* could have carried a dead body this far from the road. Still, when they finally arrived at the scene, they could see that the earth had been freshly turned. Finding it too dark to dig that night, an officer was left to guard the grave until the next morning.

Returning at dawn, police carefully began excavating the site, only to discover that it was not a grave at all, but a freshly laid pipeline. Although not greatly surprised, it was still a major disappointment to those searching for the missing girl.

~*~*~

District Attorney Raymond Reid hung up the phone, leaned back in his chair, and sighed with disgust. That had been the umpteenth call he had fielded that day, all from angry residents who demanded to know why the police hadn't found Helen Moyer yet. The public had been breathing down Reid's neck for days, and he knew it was only a matter of time before the press would start too. He feared that the media would soon begin ridiculing the police for their handling of the investigation, and their inability to find the missing girl, and he was loathe to see that happen. Reid wanted this case solved, and he wanted it solved now.

Later that afternoon, the prosecutor met with the Coatesville investigators, county detectives, and the Pennsylvania State Police, and laid out the strategy he wanted them to take in the case.

"I want this investigation centered on Modena and Coatesville," Reid told the men. "I'm convinced this girl was hit accidentally, and the driver carried her body away to conceal it, and I think he lives in the vicinity of either Modena of Coatesville. It's possible he carried her body a great distance away, but it's just as likely that he dug a hole in his cellar and buried her there." Either way, Reid continued, it was his belief that the solution to the case would be found either where Helen lived, or where she went to school, and he wanted the investigation focused on those two areas.

State Police Lieutenant Edwin Griffith had watched as the investigation into Helen's disappearance led nowhere, but he knew it wasn't because the police were slacking in their efforts. They were following up every clue that came in, but Griffith realized there was a lack of organization in the investigation. It was his belief that the answer to the puzzle lay somewhere amid the stacks of information they had already collected. They just needed to organize what they had and connect the dots.

State Police Major Lynn Adams had recently told the press that he expected the case to be solved within a week, but admitted there was still no clear indication of what had happened to the girl. Helen might have been abducted, or the victim of a hit and run, Adams said, or, she might "have run away and staged the scene herself to throw searchers off her scent."

Griffith had to agree that he wasn't sure himself which theory fit the Moyer disappearance, but he believed the evidence they had already gathered would tell them. With those thoughts in mind, the frustration of District Attorney Reid, and the fact that local residents had given up searching for the missing girl, Griffith decided to take command of the investigation himself.

The first thing the Lieutenant did was to start backtracking over the entire case. He had never believed that Helen had run away, and as he began separating and correlating tips, phone messages, and witness statements, he came to believe that he was right. There was a pattern emerging; of that he was sure.

For instance, police had received a call from a man who related that his father-in-law, William Parry, had seen a green truck with a broken headlight near the town of Glenmoore. Parry had told his daughter about it, who had told her husband, who had called the police. That call had prompted authorities to request a list of all registered owners of green trucks in Chester County.

In going through all the tips police had gathered pertaining to green trucks, Griffith soon found another message, this one from a man named Herman Reed, who had seen a young man repairing a broken headlight on a green truck the same night Helen disappeared. Reed, however, had added something else: the owner of the green trucks name. The truck didn't belong to the youth who had been repairing it, Reed said, but to the boy's father, O. Jackson Meyer. A quick look at the list of registered owners of green trucks in Chester County revealed Meyer's name on it.

Griffith ordered a discreet inquiry into O. Jackson Meyer, a well-respected and quite wealthy businessman in the town, and learned that the man had no criminal record. The same, however, could not be said for O. Jackson's nineteen-year-old son, Alexander, the boy seen repairing the headlight on the green truck.

Despite his youth, Alexander Meyer was familiar to law enforcement and had a criminal record for violence against women. He had served time in the Huntingdon Reformatory for viciously attacking two of them, and had several other minor infractions on his record.

Not wanting to alert their quarry, police didn't speak to Alex Meyer, or his family, but instead began interviewing those who worked for O. Jackson on his 500 acre farm. Those inquiries revealed that Alex had been absent from home on the day Helen disappeared, and that later that night he was observed filing down a large headlight lens to fit a lamp on his green truck. When a female worker had asked what had happened to the vehicle, Alex had allegedly gotten angry and looked extremely nervous.

The next day, February 12—the day after Helen disappeared—the truck was taken to a garage to have some repair work done, unusual since the vehicle was brand new and had only been purchased two weeks earlier. A talk with the garage mechanic revealed that the 1937, ¾-ton, green Ford pick-up, with less than 3,000 miles on it, had been brought in by Alex Meyer. The truck bore damage to the hood and right headlight, as well as several long scratches down the passenger-side door.

Griffith was amazed by how quickly the pieces were falling into place, and when a young girl of about twenty-years-old appeared at the state trooper barracks, he soon realized that he had found the icing for his cake.

The woman told the investigators that she had been stopped several times on Modena Road by a man in a green truck who always asked if she wanted a ride. The man was insistent, the woman said, and had once even offered her $5.00 to get in his truck. She had never accepted his invitations, however, and eventually the man had always driven off. The description she gave of the man closely matched that of all the other girls who had been offered rides: young, husky, clean cut, with dark hair and a baby face. The description fit Alexander Meyer perfectly, and so did the woman's assumption that the man worked on a farm because his truck often carried feed bags in the bed. Meyer was known to work for his father delivering both milk and feed with the green truck.

The most startling aspect of the girl's story came, however, when she was asked when she had last had an encounter with this man. "It was last Thursday afternoon," the woman said softly, beginning to cry, "Only a few hours before Helen disappeared."

It was time, Griffith knew, to take a much closer look at Alex Meyer.

~*~*~

Alexander Thweatt Meyer was born to O. Jackson Meyer and his wife, Louise, in Wallace Township, Pennsylvania, just north of the city of Downingtown. If anything could be said about the Meyer family, it was that they had plenty of money. In fact, O. Jackson Meyer was filthy rich. The family lived on a palatial estate in a luxurious house situated on a 500 acre working farm. O. Jackson had not made his fortune as a farmer but rather in the coal industry, working as a broker for a Philadelphia firm.

Although the Meyers were well-respected and friendly in the community, they weren't overly close with many people, preferring to maintain their privacy which they cherished. O. Jackson's life revolved around his work, and Louise's around her family. The couple had everything money could buy and they were generous with their children, lavishing them with toys and games when they were young, and clothing, vacations, and cars when they grew up. In fact, O. Jackson had just purchased the new, green, Ford truck for Alex to use on the family farm.

Little Alex was an active baby who eventually grew to be an undisciplined and spoiled child. If truth be told, the boy was a brat and a bully from a young age. When he began attending the Wallace Seminary, a small country school near his home, he found it difficult to make friends with either classmates or teachers, and by 1927, the boy's behavior had become so bad at the school that O. Jackson was forced to pull him out and enroll him at Downingtown Junior High. Downingtown was a private school, and the Meyers were required to pay tuition to have their eleven-year-old son attend there. They had hopes that his behavior would improve, but that was not the case. They quickly found that nothing had changed with the boy's behavior or attitude.

Dr. Donald Campbell, the principal of Downingtown Junior High, later claimed that Meyer was "a confirmed trouble-maker and truant" while he was enrolled there. It wasn't only trouble that Alex sought, however, but attention as well.

"He would do anything to get attention," said Anna Hall, one of his teachers. "He was one of the most difficult persons to discipline I ever saw." Although Hall admitted that Alex never actually disobeyed an order, "he always tried to evade it," she said.

Alex was not a good student, and seemed not to care about anything: not his fellow classmates or his teachers, and certainly not his grades. He wasn't a stupid boy, but he was lazy and arrogant and felt that as a Meyer, he was above everyone else and didn't have to do anything he chose not to.

"His trouble was lack of effort, rather than lack of natural intelligence," said another of his teachers, Ida Lillard. "He was a constant trouble-maker, but on the few occasions when he really tried, he showed ready ability to master the work."

Alex, however, rarely tried. He had to repeat the sixth grade twice, and then also the seventh grade twice. When he was told that he had failed the eighth grade as well, and would need to repeat it, Alex finally gave up. He was sixteen-years-old and had no intention of being in the eighth grade when others his age were getting ready to graduate. Besides, he didn't think he needed an education. He had always worked on his father's farm, and figured he always would. After all, one day he would be rich himself, when he and his siblings inherited the family fortune.

It was a reasonable assumption on the boy's part. One day he would get married, have children, and become part owner of O. Jackson's farm. But there was one small glitch in that scenario that Alexander Meyer was well aware of; girls just didn't seem to cotton to him.

Alex wasn't sure why that was. He considered himself good-looking enough, with dark hair and a muscular build, and he took pride in always keeping himself neatly groomed and dressing flashy. He took pains to present an air of wealth and sophistication about himself, and thought he had everything needed to instantly attract members of the opposite sex. And he was right. Alex attracted girls easily, but the moment he opened his mouth, most of them ran for the hills.

Alex was cocky, brazen, and arrogant; a braggart who looked down on most people and constantly boasted about his family's wealth and possessions. He bragged of owning forty suits—attire for any occasion—of the money his father made, the jewelry his mother wore, and the vehicles the family drove. He gloated about the expensive vacations they took and the cost to keep up their magnificent home. He talked disdainfully of those he considered poorer than himself, and ridiculed anyone who had to work for what they needed.

Alex's braggadocio turned everyone off and made him unpopular with girls and boys alike. He had few friends, and throughout his entire nineteen years, there were only two occasions when females accompanied him on what could be considered a date. Besides his bragging, however, most of those who knew him regarded Alex as something of an odd duck. The boy was strange, often said things that made little sense, and laughed when it was inappropriate to do so, such as when someone got hurt or misfortune befell them.

Even his own parents seemed to know their son had problems, although it was something they undoubtedly rarely discussed with others. At one point, after Alex had quit school, O. Jackson sent his son to West Virginia to work in a coal mine, perhaps hoping the experience would do him good and straighten the boy out. It didn't, however, and soon enough Alex was back in Pennsylvania and working on the family farm.

In July of 1934, when Alex was seventeen, two young girls from Philadelphia, Anna Blasch, also seventeen, and Viola Bauder, nineteen, were visiting relatives in Glenmoore, a small town located ten miles north of Coatesville. On the afternoon of July 22, Anna and Viola made plans to go hiking in the woods, eat a picnic lunch, and then go for a swim—three things they rarely got to experience while living in the city. The two girls headed out around noon, carrying their picnic lunch as they walked along a lonely dirt road, chatting happily. The girls loved coming to the country, and always marveled at the difference between it and the cement jungle of the city they were used to. After walking a short distance, the two girls could hear the sound of a car motor approaching from behind, and soon a dark sedan pulled alongside them. There was a nice-looking dark-haired youth leaning over from behind the wheel, smiling at them through the open passenger window.

"Do you need a ride?" Alexander Meyer called in a friendly voice.

Anna and Viola both shook their heads and told him no, then watched as the youth gave them a wave and drove away. Neither girl thought too much of the encounter, but within ten minutes they both saw the same car coming back towards them from the opposite direction. Again, Meyer stopped and asked the girls if they were sure he couldn't give them a lift. Again the two girls refused and the boy drove on.

Anna and Viola watched as the car disappeared from view, and then began to giggle. The boy obviously "liked" one of them, and they teased each other about which it might be. Their joking quickly dissipated, however, when, for the third time in less than twenty minutes, the same car with the smiling driver rolled to a stop beside them once again. The driver was no longer smiling, and his manner was much more gruff and insistent. He didn't ask them if they needed a ride, but demanded that they get into his car. Anna and Viola, feeling uncomfortable and slightly afraid, again refused, and noticed a flash of anger cross the boy's eyes at their words. It scared the two girls, who quickly began walking away. They were anxious for the boy to leave, but Meyer simply sat there for a few moments, the car idling on the road, before finally flooring the engine and speeding away, the tires kicking up a cloud of dirt and stones in their wake.

Hoping to have finally gotten rid of their stalker, Anna and Viola walked a little further down the road and then veered off into the woods. They were still discussing the strange young man in the car when suddenly a shot rang out, piercing the stillness of the forest, and causing both girls to stop in their tracks. To Anna Blasch, the shot sounded like it had come from a cap gun and she looked around, trying to see who had fired it. Suddenly another shot rang out and Anna saw Viola pitch forward and fall to the ground. Shocked, Anna stood still, unable to move as she watched a crimson pool of blood gush from her friend's head. Then something hit her as well, and everything went black.

Anna had no idea how long she was unconscious, but she awoke to find the young man from the car dragging her into some bushes. She saw that Viola was already lying in the shrubbery, her clothing in disarray, and terrified, the injured girl began to struggle and scream. Luckily, her cries attracted the attention of a neighboring farmer, Jesse Thompson, who happened to be driving by.

Thompson screeched to a halt when he heard the screams, and leapt from his car just as a furious Alexander Meyer took off running. Thompson, shocked upon discovering the two gravely injured girls, hurriedly carried them to his car and sped off towards the local hospital.

At the same time, Alexander Meyer returned to his own car, which he had concealed farther down the road in a stand of tree, and headed back towards town. He had only gone a short distance when Jim Taggert,* a boy he knew from school, flagged him down. Taggert had heard the shots, and had seen Jesse Thompson tearing out of the area. When he saw Alex Meyer coming from the same direction, Taggert flagged him down to see what was going on. Alex appeared nervous and was sweating profusely, but he nodded and pointed back in the direction from which he had just come. "Two girls got shot down the road," he said excitedly. Before Taggert could ask for any details, however, Meyer quickly drove away.

Both girls were still alive when Thompson reached the hospital, and a call was immediately placed to the police. County Detective Francis Grubb, who was later assigned an active role in the disappearance of Helen Moyer, was the first officer to respond. Arriving at the hospital, Grubb found Anna Blasch alive and conscious, and able to give a detailed description of her and Viola's attacker. Heading out to the scene of the attack, Grubb found a bunch of people milling around the road, trying to locate where the shooting had occurred. Among the crowd was Jim Taggert, who told the detective he had learned of what had happened from Alexander Meyer. Grubb asked what Meyer looked like, and Taggert provided a description that matched that of the man Anna Blasch had described.

There was no need for Grubb to ferret out an address for the boy; everyone knew where the estate of O. Jackson Meyer was located. And so, armed with the information that O. Jackson's son knew about the shooting long before he possibly could have, Grubb drove directly to their house.

Alex was not there, however, nor were any other members of his family. Learning from one of their farmhands that the Meyers had left to visit Carsonia Park, a popular amusement park near Reading. Grubb requested back-up and then drove to the park with his men and began searching for Alex. They eventually found him splashing around in a swimming pool, having a grand old time, and looking like he hadn't a care in the world.

As Grubb placed the boy under arrest, in front of the other swimmers and his stunned parents, Alex did not protest, and left willingly with the detective. Grubb drove the boy directly to the hospital, where he found Viola Bauder had also regained consciousness. From their hospital beds, both girls identified Alex as their attacker. After that, Alex readily admitted the shootings to Grubb, and told him that he was angry because the girls had refused to ride with him.

Returning to the scene of the crime, Meyer showed the detective where he had parked his car and then waited behind a clump of bushes for the girls to walk by. When they did, he said, he had fired three shots, two of which hit each girl in the head.

It was nothing short of a miracle that both girls survived their attack. Each had been shot in the head, and while Anna was seriously injured, Viola was much worse—the bullet that struck her had actually touched her brain. Anna spent two weeks in the hospital recuperating and Viola an entire month. Although both girls physically recovered from their injuries, they would carry the mental scars of their ordeal with them for the rest of their lives.

Alex was housed in the Chester County jail to await trial and eventually, six months later, on January 17, 1935, pled guilty to the attempted murder of Anna and Viola. Judge Butler Windle sentenced the boy to "an indeterminate term" at the Huntingdon Reformatory, calling the crime one of the most "heinous" he had seen in the county's history. Alex, upon hearing the judge's sentence, broke down and cried.

Incarcerated at the reformatory—and locked up with some of the toughest youths in the state—Alex was no longer the bully he had once been. Timid and afraid, the boy kept mainly to himself and became something of a model prisoner. Although there were a few minor infractions to mar his record at Huntingdon, most were from altercations he had not started. While Alex was in prison, O. Jackson and Louise visited him regularly, and their support for their son never wavered.

All of this contributed to the parole board's decision to release Alexander Meyer after he had served only fourteen months for the attempted murder of the two teenage girls. Alex was paroled in September of 1936—only five months before Helen Moyer disappeared—and moved back in with his parents. Once again, he began working for his father on the family farm, where he tried to maintain a low profile and get on with his life. O. Jackson and Louise worried about their son and tried to do what they could for him. Only two weeks before Helen vanished, O. Jackson bought the new 1937 green Ford truck believing it might help if the boy had a reliable vehicle to use in his daily tasks.

~*~*~

In the early morning hours of February 20, 1937, local and state police arrived outside the Meyer farm and watched as nineteen-year-old Alex helped load milk into his father's new green truck. It was Alex's job to deliver the milk each morning, and around 5:30 am, the youth pulled away from the barn and headed down the driveway. Tailing him at a distance, several state troopers and local police followed him to the Philadelphia suburb of Wayne, where they were met by other investigators from the Harrisburg and Reading State Police barracks.

At one point, when Alex slowed down near a stop sign, State Trooper C. M. Ross hopped on the back of the truck and rode along with him unobserved. The two traveled for about a mile before ten police cars converged on the truck and took Meyer into custody. They returned to Coatesville, where Alex was taken to the local police station and subjected to questioning.

Confronted with the evidence police had gathered against him, Alexander Meyer quickly admitted that he had run Helen Moyer down with his milk truck, but he insisted it was an accident. He had panicked, he said, and took the girl's body to conceal it.

"Where is she?" Captain Ralph Williams of the Coatesville Police asked, feeling relieved that the case was about to be resolved.

"I left her on a farm near my house," Alex answered. "I can show you."

After being placed in a squad car, Meyer began giving directions. He had the investigators drive out to his house and then continue on about a half mile farther up the road. Alex said he had hidden Helen's body at the old Guthrie place—a piece of property adjoining the lower edge of his father's farm. The police were familiar with the place and knew that there was an old abandoned farmhouse there, dilapidated and in need of great repair. When they turned into the driveway, Alex directed them to drive around back. He got out of the car and surveyed the scene, looking almost nostalgic as he did so.

"Well," Captain Williams asked impatiently, "where is she?"

Alex paced off about ten feet and then stopped, pointing farther beyond. "In there," he said, gesturing.

Captain Williams didn't know what "in there," meant; there was nothing there other than a few trees that bordered an open field and a large pile of fieldstone. "Where?" he asked again, confused.

Meyers took a step closer and pointed towards the fieldstone. "In there," he said. "She's in there."

"You mean you piled all that rock on her?" Williams asked, horrified.

Alex shook his head. "It's not a pile of rocks," he explained. "It's a well. I threw her down the well and then dynamited over it to cover her up."

The officers at the scene stood in stunned disbelief, rendered speechless by Alex's words, which had been spoken in a casual and unworried manner. My God, Captain Williams thought as he stared at the huge pile of rubble, how would they ever recover Helen's body, if, indeed, there was anything left *to* recover?

Meyer was taken back to police headquarters where he was questioned further while state and local police began organizing a team of investigators to excavate the collapsed well. It was more difficult, however, than any of them had imagined. Realizing that it was going to take a hell of a lot more manpower than they had, several officers went into town to round up some volunteers.

By late that afternoon, the men had removed more than 1,000 pounds of rock and rubble, and finally exposed the opening to the well. It was an eerie looking tomb, a pitch black vertical shaft measuring 75 feet deep and lined with piled field stone.

No one wanted to think about descending into that pit, and no one volunteered to do so until a farmer by the name of Orville Mann stepped forward and offered to go. Using ropes and a ladder, they lowered Mann into the well, where he remained only a few minutes before calling to those on top to pull him back up. By then a large crowd had gathered, and when Orville Mann finally came into view, everyone was shocked to see him holding the nude and mutilated body of a young girl, presumably sixteen-year-old Helen Moyer. Had the authorities envisioned how truly awful it was going to be, they would have sent the crowd away before allowing Mann to come up.

~*~*~

Back in Coatesville, Alexander Meyer continued to insist that Helen's death had been an accident. He had not hit her deliberately, he said, but had not seen her until it was too late. The police knew Meyer's background, however, and when word came from the old Guthrie place regarding the condition of Helen's body, they doubted his "accident" story even more.

The body was in horrible shape. Besides the obvious fractures, wounds, and gashes, Helen's left leg had been dismembered below the knee. While it was arguable that those injuries could have occurred from the vehicle strike or the explosion in the well, the ligature marks around Helen's neck, and the fact that she was nude, could not be explained so easily.

When Assistant District Attorney Philip Reilly confronted Meyer with those facts, the youth seemed to consider his words for a moment before simply shrugging his shoulder.

"Okay," Alex said calmly, "I did it."

"Did what?" Reilly asked carefully.

"I hit her on purpose and killed her."

When asked why, Alex shrugged again and said simply, "I'd been thinking for weeks about how I could get a girl, and I knew that a lot of them walked home from the Coatesville High School. So I drove around looking for one who was alone, and the first one I saw was the Moyer girl. I hit her at about 45 mph, pulled her into the cab, and took her to the old house."

"Okay, Alex," Reilly said, stopping him before he could go further. "Let's start at the beginning."

In the room with Meyer and the Assistant District Attorney was Edwin Musser, warden of the Chester County Jail, and Charles Cook, the West Chester constable. At that time, Reilly also had Hallowell Lewis, the court stenographer called in. When everyone was assembled, Reilly nodded at the prisoner.

"Whenever you're ready, Alex, just go ahead and start at the beginning." And Alexander Meyer did.

He had woken early on the morning of Thursday, February 11, 1937 Alex said, and, since he didn't have to deliver milk that day, spent the morning doing chores around the farm. After lunch, he drove to Glenmoore in his green milk truck to pick up two loads of coal from Schell's Feed Store. After unloading the coal at his home, he drove to the Ford Agency in Downingtown, about seven miles away. There, he picked up a load of poultry equipment that had been delivered for his brother. By the time he loaded the equipment, which consisted of four poultry Brooder stoves, the back of his truck bed was completely filled. The Brooder stoves came in two pieces, the boy explained, so instead of four cases in the truck there were actually eight.

"My brother's an agent for these stoves," Alex said proudly, "and when he sells one, he has the company deliver it to different locations around here. I help him out by picking them up for him."

"That's very nice of you." Reilly said, and Alex beamed.

Continuing on, the boy said that after the truck bed was full, he drove out to the Lincoln Highway and turned left at the light. He drove up the hill and then took the road that branches off to the left which brought him out on Modena Road. He claimed he had not been on the road since "I met the girl with her little brother several weeks ago," although Jennie Watterson had been attacked there only a week before Helen disappeared.

Alex continued by saying that when he drove down Modena Road on that day, February 11, initially he had seen no one except for a few Bell Telephone workers.

"I saw the telephone truck, and the men working," Alex said, "but I don't know what they were doing. I was in a hurry. See, there's no set time for us to eat supper at my house, but we always eat as soon as my father gets home." His worried tone as he talked made it clear that he was expected home for dinner whenever the family sat down to eat.

When Reilly asked if Alex remembered seeing William Crawford, the scrap worker who had noticed the green truck sideswipe the telephone pole, Meyer shook his head. "I was traveling down the road, going about 45 miles per hour," he said, "but I don't recall passing anyone going in either direction." But, he added, it was as he began coming towards the curve that he first saw the girl.

Alex hesitated for a moment, then explained to his interrogators what had happened.

"You see," he began, "when I left Coatesville, my purpose was to go down to Modena to get some girl. I had no particular girl in mind—just any girl—and when I first saw this girl, my mind wasn't really made up. She was walking along the edge of the concrete, on the right hand side of the road. She was going south, in the same direction as the truck, and on the same side of the road, and when I first saw her, she was about thirty-five to forty feet away."

Again he paused, as if reluctant to go on.

"What happened when you saw her?" Reilly encouraged him.

Alex sighed audibly before finishing his story in a rush. "Like I said, when I first saw her, my mind wasn't really made up, but when I got fairly close to her, I swerved and hit her, purposely driving my truck against her."

The impact flung the girl onto the hood, and then propelled her over the top of the truck. "She landed in the back, on the road," Meyer said, "and I stopped the truck, got out, and went to her. I knew she was dead, so I placed her on the front seat alongside of me, turned the truck around, and started back to Coatesville. But when I turned around, I backed into something."

Meyer said that on the trip back to Coatesville, he passed the Bell Telephone people again, and they were just leaving the area. It was then, he said, that he felt the girl's wrist for a pulse, but "I didn't feel any beat there." Scared, the boy then decided to drive towards his house which was located northeast of Modena Road. He hadn't gone all the way to Coatesville, he said, but had turned to his right just before reaching the city. Once back on the Lincoln Highway, he had quickly driven towards Downingtown.

"Was Helen alive during this time?" Reilly asked. "Do you know?"

Alex shrugged. "The girl was alongside me all this time, but I did nothing to determine her condition after that first time," he said casually.

Those in the room noticed that the prisoner never referred to Helen by name. He called her "the girl", or "she;" and at one time, "the Moyer girl," but he never referred to her as Helen.

From Downingtown, Meyer continued, he took Route 5 toward Honeybrook, turned left, "and went out as far as that old church there, just this side of Guthrieville." From there he traveled to Lyndell, where he turned left, went across the bridge, and drove up to his house.

"I didn't see anyone at home," he said, sounding relieved, "so I drove past the house and went up to the old Guthrie place which is about half a mile farther up the road. I stopped the truck right by the house and took her body out—she was fully clothed then. I lifted her in my arms and carried her around the back of the house near the well, which is about fifty feet away, and then I stripped her—took all her clothing off."

Asked if he had taken her into the house to strip her, Meyer shook his head no, indicating that he had stripped her right there in the yard. Reilly shivered involuntarily, remembering how bitterly cold it was that day.

"I was out in the open at this time, and she had nothing on but her stockings. It was then that I attacked her."

"You had sex with her?" one of the men asked.

Meyer nodded in agreement. "I raped her," he said softly, dropping his eyes to the table. "She was dead at the time."

The room was silent for a moment, and then Alexander Meyer looked up at his interrogators and smiled—actually smiled—before continuing with his story. It was as if he were chatting with a couple of old friends, his questioners thought, finding his demeanor grotesquely bizarre.

"I was only about ten feet from the well," Alex said, "so I carried her over to it and dropped her in. I then picked up all her clothing—which was lying on the ground—and dropped that in the well also. Then I went home and had dinner with my family. It was already dark, and I didn't say anything to anyone after I got home."

The next day, Meyer said, he read about the girl in the paper but still didn't say anything to anyone. Then, as if answering a question, although none had been asked, Alex blurted out, "You know, I had as good a chance of seeing a girl on that road as on any other road."

Asked how badly he had damaged his truck when he hit the girl, Meyer said the right headlight was broken and there was a dent in the right front fender and the right side of the hood. There was also a long scratch down the passenger side from when he hit the pole.

"When did you dynamite the well?"

"The next day," Meyer answered. He had gotten the dynamite from his father's car, it having been purchased to remove stumps from their property. He took the explosives back to the Guthrie place to "cover it up—fill the well in over the body."

"I couldn't see the girl when I looked in there," he said, "but I put two sticks of dynamite in between the rocks, down in the well as far as I could reach."

"How far down?" Reilly asked.

The boy thought about it for a moment. "About three feet, I guess. I was holding the fuse, which was about a foot long, when I put the dynamite into the well. I used the same fuse for both sticks of dynamite." He said he then stood "about fifty or sixty feet away when the explosion occurred. Actually," he corrected himself, "it was two explosions."

He admitted he didn't go back to the well after that, but instead simply went home. "I didn't bother to go see whether it covered it up. I didn't want to go back."

"Weren't you afraid of someone hearing the explosion? Seeing it?" Warden Musser asked.

Meyer shook his head and smiled. "There was a lot of smoke," he admitted, "but I wasn't worried about the explosion because the rock quarry was on the other side of the hill."

"Did you ever go back to that well, Alex?"

Alex shook his head. "I wouldn't have been able to see anything if I did go back anyway."

Reilly decided to change the subject and ask Alex about the attack on Jennie Watterson.

Yes, Alex said, he had been on the Modena Road when he saw "the girl"—again refusing to use his victim's name—walking along the road near the Coatesville School. "I stopped the car and asked her if she wanted a lift, and she got in. But just before we got to Modena, I hit her with a screwdriver that had been laying on the seat. She yelled, and when I went to make a turn, she jumped out and I went after her. I stopped because she was running towards a house."

Reilly was glad to have the confession to Jennie Watterson's attack, although he didn't need it. Jennie had already been brought to the station where she observed Alex Meyer in secret, and identified him as her attacker.

Those taking the youth's confession were shocked by his calm, cool, and carefree manner. Alexander Meyer seemed no more concerned about hitting Helen Moyer with his truck, than if it had been a chipmunk or a squirrel that he had struck. In fact, the only time he seemed to get upset was when his interrogators asked if he wanted to see his mother.

"No!" Alex said forcefully and coldly. "No. Absolutely not."

When Hallowell Lewis finished taking his confession, Reilly slid it across the table and asked Alex to sign it. Much to his surprise, however, the youth refused. He could not sign it, Alex said, until he spoke with his father, but he wanted to do that at home, not here.

Reilly decided to acquiesce to the boy's demand. Rather than bring O. Jackson to him, they'd take Alex out to his house. There was always the chance that seeing his old homestead, and knowing he would no longer be living there, might produce some type of reaction in the boy.

Alex spent a short time secreted in his father's study with O. Jackson before leaving the room in tears. He was then returned to Coatesville where he agreed to sign his statement.

It had been a long day, but despite their weariness, those who had listened to Alexander Meyer's confession knew they would not sleep any time soon. They found Alex so strange, so unsettling in his words and his unresponsive behavior that after he was taken to the Chester County jail one of his interrogators gave the following statement to the press. "Meyer has no interest in what's happening to him. There's just a trace of sullenness about him. He's not stupid, but he *is* a sexual pervert of some sort. On some matters, he's plenty smart."

Other than his temporary disdain towards his mother, Alex had shown emotion only once that day. It had happened shortly after he completed his confession, when a photographer came by the room and asked if he'd pose for a photo. Alex, his face turning red with anger, sat up straighter in his chair and glared. "If I had a shotgun," he shouted, "I'd blow you to hell!"

~*~*~

Orville Mann, in describing the recovery of Helen's body, told the authorities that it had been resting in two feet of muddy water on the bottom of the well. The police knew they would need Mann's help again to go back into that black pit and see if he could find more evidence but first, the well would need to be shored up and roped off. The explosions had made it unstable, and the hundreds of people who had flocked to the old farmhouse were at risk of collapsing the entire thing.

When police finally felt it safe enough for Orville Mann to re-enter the well, the helpful farmer once again descended to the depths of Helen Moyer's makeshift tomb. The search proved fruitless, although Mann did tell investigators that he thought he might have felt some clothing, but there was too much mud and water in the well to be sure. Realizing they would need to pump the well out before anything else could be found, police abandoned their search for the night.

~*~*~

When word of Alexander Meyer's confession was leaked, the public's reaction was almost as explosive as the dynamite he had used to try and conceal his crime. To think that this monster had deliberately run over the girl, raped her after she was dead, and then tossed her body in an abandoned well incensed the towns of Modena and Coatesville. Feelings ran so high in the community that there were calls for the killer's immediate lynching, a threat the police were taking all too seriously. Only twenty years earlier, Coatesville had been the site of one of the most gruesome lynchings on record.

It occurred on August 13, 1911, when Zachariah Walker, a black iron worker, shot and killed special policeman Edgar Rice. Walker, who fled on foot, was found a few hours later hiding in a cherry tree. When a posse of men surrounded the tree, the terrified Walker placed his pistol in his mouth and pulled the trigger. The suicide attempt was unsuccessful, however, and Walker, still alive and conscious, was immediately rushed to Coatesville Hospital where doctors strapped him down and shackled him to a cot while attempting to treat him.

Three hours later, a group of about fourteen men cut the hospital phone lines, forced their way inside, picked up the cot with Walker still tied and shackled to it, and carried it away into the night. The men drove about ten miles to a secluded farm outside of the city, and there, amidst a crowd of about 2,000 men, women, and children, set the injured man on fire.

It was estimated that up to 5,000 people heard Walker's horrifying screams and cries for mercy as the flames seared the flesh from his body, but no one stepped forward to help. When the fire began to cool down, several men demolished a nearby fence and used the posts to fuel it. Three times, after his ropes had burned through, Walker attempted to get away from the inferno, and three times men rushed forward to push him back down.

When, mercifully, his ordeal was finally over, there was literally nothing left to the man; Zachariah Walker had been burned to a crisp. Fifteen local men and boys were eventually indicted for Walker's lynching, but each was acquitted of all charges.

Now, with Alexander Meyer, police were seeing the same reaction to his crime as they had witnessed with Zachariah Walker's. They immediately beefed up security on Meyer, both inside and outside of the jail. Guards were placed around the building, and prisoners were denied their radios so they wouldn't know who Meyer was.

Even Absalom Moyer seemed concerned for the welfare of his daughter's killer when he agreed to give a statement to the press. Helen's father urged people to leave justice to the police. "It's not my place to say what should be done with him [Meyer]," Absalom said. "That's up to the law."

The Meyer family was dealing with their own fears for Alex, and secluded themselves at their private estate. Only once did any member speak to the press, and that was O. Jackson.

The strain of the ordeal evident on his face, Alex's father spoke in an emotional voice when he said, "It is clearly a mental case. We believe we did what we could for the boy. The whole family is in terrible shape from the shock of the thing and I know you'll excuse me from talking about it anymore."

It was not only Meyer, however, who came under the scrutiny of the public and press, but Huntingdon Reformatory as well. It seemed if Alex were a monster, then his lair was the reformatory. When word leaked out that psychiatrists at the institution had labeled Meyer "sub-normal" long before he was released, the people of Modena and Coatesville howled with rage. How could Huntingdon have let this boy out after spending less than two years there for shooting and nearly killing two other young girls? It was a question that demanded an answer, and one the institution was forced to respond to.

Secretary of Welfare and Superintendent of Huntingdon, John D. Pennington, immediately defended himself and the reformatory's decision to release Alex.

"Alexander Meyer was not sub-normal," Pennington said with conviction. "He responded well to discipline, had a good home with a father financially able to care for him, a promise of a job in Chester County, and sponsorship of the Child Guidance Clinic in Philadelphia. With full knowledge of the clinic's action and of the personality of the boy, I recommended his parole to the board of trustees and I assume full responsibility."

Two days later, however, after Pennington had come under a barrage of heavy criticism, he quickly tried to back-peddle, this time shifting the blame for Alex's release to the Commonwealth of Pennsylvania itself. "Meyer was not sub-normal in his intellect, nor in academic or trade achievements," Pennington insisted once again, but he went on to qualify that statement by adding, "However, despite his average intelligence, he may be classed as a defective delinquent, and for the care and treatment of this class of criminal the state of Pennsylvania has made no provision."

Continuing to try and distance himself—and the reformatory—from the guilt and blame of Meyer's release, Pennington went on. "As far as human study of that boy is concerned, everything within reason was done by the officials who permitted his release. It is my conviction that no element of provision or planning was neglected in the parole of Meyer by the classification clinic of the institution. Thousands of men and women are paroled each year from penal and correctional institutions in this state and it need not be forgotten that the parole system has satisfied every reasonable expectation *when the inadequate provision which the state has made for parole supervision is considered.*"

He concluded his statement with an ominous finish. "Not abolition, but strengthening of the system is indicated. The only alternative to the parole system is a vast increase in the number of institutions."

~*~*~

On February 22, 1937, with the well on the Guthrie place pumped clear of water, Orville Mann was once again groping around on its muddy bottom. Near him rested a bucket into which he hoped to put not only Helen's clothing, but the missing pieces of her body as well. Police were curious to see if the old farmer might find something else in his search; perhaps other victims who also rested at the bottom of that black pit.

Alexander Meyer had already shot, and attempted to kill, two teenage girls. He had confessed to attacking Jennie Watterson with a screwdriver. He had attempted to abduct at least three other girls—one of them only six-years-old—and he had admitted to raping and murdering Helen Moyer. These were the victims of Alex Meyer that police knew about; was it so far-fetched to think that there might be more they were not aware of?

In questioning people who knew the boy, authorities learned that Meyer spent a lot of time around the old Guthrie place. He was seen there only a few days before Helen disappeared, and on one occasion, neighbors saw him arrive at the farm with a suspicious-looking, canvas covered box in the bed of his truck.

There was also the unknown woman discovered dead near the Meyer property five years earlier. Police had determined that the woman had been murdered and then dumped at that location, but the body was so badly decomposed that they were unable to identify her. The case had frustrated local lawmen for years, and remained unsolved.

Local police, however, were not the only ones looking into the activities of Alexander Meyer. The Pennsylvania State Police received a call from Buffalo, New York, inquiring about Alex, and requesting his picture. New York police were struggling with their own case; the murder of eighteen-year-old Mary Ellen Babcock, who was found beaten and stabbed to death in a field on February 6.

It was fast becoming clear to Pennsylvania lawmen that Alexander Meyer was unlike any other criminal they had ever dealt with. They had no way of knowing—because the term wouldn't be coined for another forty years—that they had probably just put an end to the beginning of a serial killer's career.

~*~*~

The sludge on the bottom of the well was cold and slimy, and reeked of an awful odor. It was dark and cramped in the tight space, and as Orville Mann continued to grope around, he began to feel uncomfortably claustrophobic. He was cursing Alexander Meyer, and thinking about what he would do if he could have just five minutes alone with him, when his hand struck something soft and pliable in the putrid muck. He tugged on it, but the wet goop held it fast, seeming reluctant to let it go. Heaving with all his might, Mann finally pulled the object free and saw that he was holding Helen Moyer's red knit sweater. He placed it in the bucket, and delved once more into the well bottom, rewarded again when he dislodged a piece of Helen's gaily flowered dress. Excited to finally be making progress, Mann once again plunged his hands into the cold, wet mire and immediately felt something solid. As he yanked it up, the mud creating a grotesque sucking sound upon its release, the old farmer was horrified to see that he was holding Helen Moyer's severed left foot. Mann dropped it into the bucket and immediately signaled those waiting above that he was coming up.

As there had been for the past two days, a large crowd was gathered at the Guthrie place, just beyond the ropes police had strung up. As they watched the investigators examine the contents of Mann's bucket, they could clearly see their expressions turn grim, and they knew that the old farmer had made some type of grisly discovery. Police, however, were not talking. Instead, one of the detectives came over and told the crowd to leave.

"There's nothing here for you to see," the officer said solemnly. "Why don't you just go home?" He was relieved to see that many decided to take his advice as they turned around and began walking away.

Despite the fact that the well at the Guthrie place was searched numerous more times, authorities found no more evidence, and no more bodies. Helen's left shin—the area from her knee to her ankle—was never recovered, and believed to have been "blown to bits," in the explosion.

~*~*~

Back at the Chester County Jail, Alexander Meyer was in a foul mood as he paced restlessly in his cell. He had met with his attorney that day—O. Jackson having hired former assistant U.S. attorney J. Paul MacElree from Philadelphia to represent him—and Alex was beginning to realize that it had been a huge mistake to confess to murdering the girl and dumping her body down the well. If he hadn't, he thought, the girl would never have been found and the police wouldn't have been able to do anything about it.

MacElree had told Meyer, while they visited, that he needed to keep his mouth shut and stop talking to the police. It was advice the accused murderer intended to take. But when MacElree informed his client that he had no intention of asking for bail, Alex seemed shocked and began to whine. He wanted out of jail, and appeared to think if he got bail he could just go home and resume his former life.

Alex seemed completely ignorant to the negative public sentiment towards him. When MacElree tried to tell him that residents' hatred towards him was so strong that they would like nothing more than to string him up and watch him suffer, Alex looked at his attorney like he was crazy.

"Alex," MacElree asked, "did you agree to re-enact the crime for the police?"

"Yeah," Alex answered, "but they cancelled it."

MacElree nodded. "Why do you think they did that? Because it was too dangerous to take you out of the jail. That's why there's such heavy guard around you, son. The people from Modena and Coatesville are very angry about what happened to Helen. I can't ask bail for you because I'm afraid if you got it, you wouldn't last a minute on the outside."

Alex nodded his head, as if finally understanding, but when the attorney continued by saying that it was for those same reasons that he also wouldn't allow Alex to attend the inquest scheduled for that night, the boy became upset once again.

It was not, however, only the public's sentiment towards him that Alex seemed oblivious too. He also seemed unaware and unconcerned of the serious nature of his crime and the actual trouble he was in. He ate well at the jail, slept soundly, and appeared normal enough to his jailers. However, Alex was strange, and no one could deny it. There was a possibility he might be facing the electric chair, yet to the jailers the only thing he seemed concerned about was the fact that if he went to prison, he wouldn't be able to wear the 15 new suits he had recently purchased.

That evening, Meyer's inquest was held in a small room at the Coatesville City Hall. So many people turned out for the hearing that they spilled out of the old building and into the streets. As promised, Alex was not in attendance.

For the first time, the Coroner's jury of six men, and everyone else in attendance, heard the horrifying details of Helen Moyer's ordeal. Doctor Michael Margolis, who had performed Helen's autopsy, revealed that the girl had suffered numerous and unimaginable injuries. She had a fractured skull and nose, a dislocated jaw, a deep gash on her head, ligature marks around her neck, a dismembered left leg, a fractured right one, and clear signs of a brutal and vicious sexual assault. As those listening squirmed in their seats at the horror of it all, the only consolation the doctor could give them was his estimation that Helen had been unconscious between four and five hours before death had finally ended her suffering.

There was more, however, and quite possibly the most horrifying aspect of the young girl's ordeal. The autopsy had revealed a pint of water in each of Helen's lungs, indisputable proof that she had been alive when thrown into the well. Despite all this damage to her body—the numerous injuries and water in her lungs—it was Margolis' opinion that Helen's death was attributed to internal injuries; specifically, a ruptured liver and shock.

The jury was out a mere three minutes before returning to find that "Alexander Meyer had deliberately murdered Helen Moyer." They ordered the youth held on a charge of first-degree murder and bound over for Grand Jury action. The jurors, however, incorporated something else into their verdict: "a condemnation of the parole system which permits convicts of the Meyer type to be at large."

It was a statement that would once again bring John D. Pennington, Superintendent of Huntingdon, into the limelight. The very next day, he faced the media again, looking tired, and weary of having to once more defend his institution's decision to release the boy.

"Meyer responded well to discipline while here," Pennington said, going on to repeat that Alex had a good home, the promise of a job, and sponsorship of the Child Guild Clinic in Philadelphia. "After a complete investigation by agents of the institution, we considered him with a perfect parole plan and his release was approved by the clinic board of the school."

Whatever excuse John Pennington might give meant little to the public. After having heard what Helen Moyer had endured, they wanted Alexander Meyer dead and, apparently, John D. Pennington hanging right beside him.

~*~*~

On February 23, 1937, District Attorney Reid announced that the Commonwealth of Pennsylvania would ask for the death penalty for Alexander Meyer, and then went on to say that despite what Doctor Margolis had claimed at the inquest, it was Reid's belief that Helen had died shortly after Meyer had struck her with his truck. It was unusual to have the prosecutor go against the medical examiner's findings, and people were upset by it. They believed that the prosecutor's words could only help Meyer avoid the electric chair, not send him to it. Wasn't it better to incense the public with the suffering Helen had endured rather than claim she died quickly from the truck hitting her?

Some thought Reid's statement had a lot to do with Margolis' claims that Helen had been unconscious for four or five hours before she died. They wondered if Reid felt that the act of necrophilia—having sex with a dead body—would incite the rage of the general public far more than the young girl receiving her injuries while unconscious.

That same day, nearly 5,000 people attended the viewing of Helen Moyer. So many flowers flanked the funeral home that they nearly spilled out onto the street. The young teen's family appeared in shock as they greeted the numerous people who stopped by to pay their respects. When it was learned that Absalom Moyer made only $60.00 a month in wages, a collection was taken up to help with the burial expenses.

The next day, Helen's funeral was held in the Hepzibah Baptist Church overlooking the peaceful Coatesville valley. Three clergymen officiated at the service: Reverend Joseph Quinn, Pastor of the church, and two other ministers, a Presbyterian and a Lutheran, who assisted him. Helen's parents and her two brothers sat sobbing uncontrollably in the front pew, facing her white coffin which was nearly hidden behind the huge stacks of flowers resting before it.

So many people attended the service that special traffic police were called in to handle the flow of vehicles that jammed the nearby streets. Helen's family had asked three of their daughter's classmates and three members of her Sunday school to serve as pall bearers, and then acknowledged her entire class by dubbing them honorary pall bearers as well.

Helen's murder had touched more souls than she, or her family, could ever have imagined, and as the young teen, who had dreamed of becoming a missionary, was finally laid to rest, those in attendance realized that their lives would never be the same.

~*~*~

While hundreds of people were gathering for Helen's funeral, Alexander Meyer was waking up after a good night's sleep, and then eating a substantial breakfast in his Chester County jail cell. Once finished, he sat back on his cot, his back against the wall, and lit a big cigar, puffing happily on it. One of his jailers, appalled by the youth's unconcerned attitude, decided to try and evoke some reaction out of him.

"Do you know they're burying Helen today?" the guard asked.

Meyer eyed the man for moment, and then took a long puff on his cigar, exhaling a few smoke rings in a cloud of sweet-smelling smoke.

The guard shook his head in disgust and began to walk away. Suddenly Meyer called out after him. "Hey!"

The guard turned back to see Alex, still puffing on his cigar, a smile lighting up his face. "I'm a little bored." Alex said, grinning broader. "Could you bring me some comics to read?"

The jailer would have liked nothing more than to reach through the bars and strangle Alexander Meyer to death, but he settled for verbally hitting the prisoner where he knew it would bother him most. "How come nobody's been out to visit you?" the jailer asked, grinning himself. "Don't your mama and papa like you either?"

It was no secret that Alex's family rarely, if ever, visited the jail, a fact that greatly upset the prisoner. The press was reporting that the Meyer's were staying in seclusion, and that O. Jackson was laid up with the "grippe," a virus-like illness similar to influenza.

The guard felt a measure of satisfaction as he watched Alex's face flush red with embarrassment, and his fists clench tightly in anger. Smiling, the guard tipped his hat at the prisoner then turned around and walked away.

~*~*~

J. Paul MacElree knew his client was doomed. There was no possible way he could get Alex acquitted of the charges leveled against him, nor did he want to. MacElree believed Meyer to be a dangerous young man, but he did not want to see him die in the electric chair. The attorney had already decided to focus his goal on saving Alex's life, and towards that end he would do whatever was necessary.

Still fearing for the prisoner's safety, authorities scheduled a secret hearing for February 24, in the office of Peace Justice R. Jones Patrick. Plans were also being finalized to transfer Meyer to the Delaware County Jail in Media, Pennsylvania, right after the proceedings.

Unlike his previous hearing, MacElree intended Meyer to be present at this one, and Detective Francis Grubb drove the prisoner the block and a half to Patrick's office in secret. Once there, however, the detective was alarmed to see a large crowd gathering. Somehow, word had leaked out—either accidentally or by design—about the hearing.

Just as he rushed his prisoner inside, Grubb noticed a number of vehicles—all filled with men—come cruising slowly down the street. The cars, and their cargo, remained in the area the entire time the hearing was being held, continuously circling the block, driving from Patrick's office, past the jail, and then back again.

Inside the building, Peace Justice Patrick heard from only one prosecution witness, Detective Grubb, who laid out the case they had built against Meyer. When it was the defense's turn, MacElree straightened his tie, rose, acknowledged his client and the judge, and then shocked the court with his words.

"The defendant," MacElree began, "as I understand the law, is not obligated at this time to enter a formal plea. Anticipating, however, his formal arraignment in open court, he now pleads guilty to the crime as charged."

An audible gasp was heard in the room, not just from the spectators, but from the prosecution, judge, and from the defendant himself. MacElree's plea came as a complete surprise to everyone, but the attorney felt he had no choice but to enter it. He knew any jury would convict his client immediately, and he believed the only hope Alex had of avoiding the electric chair was to plead guilty, and throw himself on the mercy of the court.

Pausing until the room settled down, MacElree continued. "I cannot and will not insult the intelligence of our county. Murder has been committed—one of the most brutal, gruesome murders of all time. In this plea, I assume my full share of responsibility acting as counsel selected by his parents and approved by the boy. I recognize no words, no regrets, nothing, can compensate Mr. and Mrs. Moyer for the death of their child. No justification can be offered, no excuse can be advanced. Perhaps in an appropriate place, at an appropriate time, an examination can be offered that, neither excusing nor justifying, may explain this terrible catastrophe."

Alex sat motionless, simmering with rage. His face bore a look of stunned disbelief. At one point, MacElree turned to give his client an encouraging smile, but his face faltered when he saw the fury radiating in Alex's eyes. Quickly turning back to the bench, the unsettled attorney continued with his speech.

"With the entering of a plea admitting guilt, the law has been vindicated. At a proper time, the court will fix punishment; the whole truth having been told by the defendant. I have an abiding faith that justice administered here shall see that an unbiased, impartial punishment shall be imposed, consistent with the purpose of the law."

When MacElree took his seat next to his client, those in the courtroom clearly heard Alex ask a question. "I'm guilty?" the boy muttered in a puzzled voice. "I'm guilty?"

Peace Justice Patrick bound Meyer's case over for the Grand Jury which was to meet on March 7, and then the hearing was over. Outside, a mob of more than 200 hundred people waited.

Highly nervous, officials abandoned their plans to move Meyer to the Delaware County jail. Those responsible for Alex had enough to worry about just trying to get him the block and a half back to the Chester County Jail. They sure in hell didn't want to risk being ambushed on the highway. After several moments of discussion, it was decided that they would surround Alex, send armed guards out in front of him, and attempt to get him out to Detective Grubb's car.

As the group moved slowly out the door, pressed so close against the prisoner that they were nearly smothering him, they were relieved to see that the crowd did absolutely nothing. There was no demonstration, no lunge for Helen's killer, not even any catcalls, only a number of glaring stares. Shortly after Meyer was secured in the back seat of the vehicle, the crowd simply dispersed and went home.

The next morning, the same guard who had watched Alex casually dismiss the funeral of Helen Moyer, again watched in disgust as the boy ate a hearty breakfast and then lit another of his huge cigars.

"Aren't you scared?" the guard suddenly asked.

"Scared of what?" Alex asked.

"Scared to get the death penalty."

Alex looked amused and then shrugged. "Aw," he said, "I'll probably get sent back to prison for another term. I'm pretty confident that it'll be nothing more than that."

~*~*~

On February 26, District Attorney Raymond Reid was asked about Meyer's plea of guilty, and the fact that the prisoner didn't seem to know his attorney was going to enter it. Reid told the press that he had no knowledge of what went on between MacElree and his client, but as for the guilty plea, he didn't expect it to be withdrawn. But, he added, "I will oppose any softening of the plea by claims of insanity."

"What are the chances he'll get death?" one of the reporters called out.

Reid hesitated for a moment. "I won't say now whether we'll press for the death sentence. I have instructed our men to go right on lining up witnesses and gathering additional evidence to be used at the trial, which will probably be held early in April."

The press was surprised. Just the day before, in open court, Reid had announced that the state *was* seeking the death penalty. They rushed off to put the district attorney's words into print, a decision that would have ramifications.

The next day, after Reid's statement went public, Governor George H. Earle received word that Alexander Meyer was to be lynched that night. Less than two hours later, Earle was told that large groups of men were reported to be gathering in Modena.

The governor was worried. He knew that Pennsylvania had not yet lived down the lynching of Zachariah Walker, and he was determined not to let such a thing happen again, especially under his watch. Placing a call to Major Lynn Adams of the Pennsylvania State Police, Earle ordered that reinforcements from Reading, Avondale, Devon and Coatesville be called out to guard the Chester County jail where Meyers was being held.

By early evening, more than fifty men armed with tear gas, shotguns, and sub-machine guns, were in place around the jail, while others were sent to search the surrounding area and nearby roads. All was quiet, however. There was no sign of the cars, supposedly loaded down with people, which were said to have already left Modena, and no indication that a mob was forming.

Adams wasn't taking any chances. He ordered his troops to stay on high alert. Anyone seen near the jail was immediately told to "move along," while Warden Musser prepared his men inside the prison for any emergency situation.

Despite all their fear and preparation, however, nothing happened. Only one person, a man seen loitering near the jail who refused to leave, was taken into custody and tossed in a cell. By 3:00 am, many of the officers had been relieved from duty and had gone home, while the rest gave a sigh of relief that, apparently, nothing drastic was going to occur.

~*~*~

As February slipped into March, the pressure on Huntingdon Reformatory continued to grow. State Senator George B. Scarlet submitted a resolution to have the parole system probed. "I have recommended a committee of five senators to investigate how the parole board determines who is released," Scarlet said. "I want to know how mental delinquents and habitual criminals secure their release from state institutions."

On March 8, the Grand Jury, after hearing from only one witness—Detective Francis Grubb, who read Meyer's confession—handed down an indictment in less than two minutes. A trial date was set for March 22, 1937.

A trial was a mere formality since Meyer had already pled guilty, and MacElree assured the press that he would not change that plea. Neither, he insisted, did he plan to enter a "not guilty by reason of insanity" plea for his client. MacElree was counting on the mercy of the court to save Alex's life.

Two judges, Butler Windle—who had sentenced Alex to Huntingdon less than two years before—and Judge Ernest Harvey had been selected to preside at the trial and each, MacElree said, "would hear testimony, fix the degree of guilt, and choose the penalty. Such a procedure, I believe, is justified by the facts, and it will permit disposition of the case in a manner becoming to the dignity of the courts."

On March 22, 1937, Alexander Meyer was escorted into the courtroom by Sheriff Fred Wahl. Perhaps he finally understood the seriousness of the charges against him, because he looked noticeably haggard and was hiding his eyes behind a pair of large dark sunglasses. Meyer had lost a considerable amount of weight, and it was said he wasn't sleeping well.

In court with Alex Meyer was his attorney, Paul MacElree, and another lawyer, Harold K. Wood, who had been hired to assist with his defense. Standing before Judge Butler Windle, Alex, pale and trembling, softly whispered, "Guilty," when asked how he pled.

"In view of the plea," Windle said, "it becomes necessary for the court to determine the degree of guilt and to fix the punishment. Before this can be done, it will be necessary for the court to hear testimony of witnesses." Windle set April 5 for the hearing, but MacElree, worried about the toll the proceedings were having on his client, quickly objected. Was it possible to hear evidence today, he asked the judge?

"It will be more satisfactory on April 5," Windle replied before banging his gavel and bringing the hearing to an end. Within five minutes of having arrived in court, Alex was back en route to the Chester County Jail.

~*~*~

Justice moved swiftly in 1937. The trial began on April 5 before Judges Butler Windle and Ernest Harvey, less than two months after Alexander Meyer killed Helen Moyer.

Helen's parents were the only members of her family to attend the hearing, joined by a close family friend who was there to lend moral support. Alex Meyer's family took up an entire bench in the back of the courtroom, barely 15 feet away from Helen's family.

In a brief opening statement, Paul MacElree admitted that Meyer was guilty of first degree murder and that "legally" the boy was sane. "But," he continued, "Alex was a victim of his own retarded mentality. He was insensible to pain, either physical or mental"

Alex was "completely normal," MacElree stressed, except when the urge for sex came upon him. "We don't dispute the fact that this is murder of the first degree, but the killing was only incidental to the other happenings." It was true, MacElree conceded, that Meyer "is not insane as the law describes or considers, but I will present evidence to show his type of mentality."

Hogwash, District Attorney Raymond Reid seemed to say as he leapt to his feet, telling the court that Alexander Meyer was nothing more than a cold-blooded killer. He was not insane, Reid said, and had complete control of his actions. Had he chosen too, Meyer could have easily stopped himself from killing Helen Moyer, but Meyer had not chosen to do that; instead, he had deliberately run the girl down and disposed of her body like nothing more than garbage. "There is no doubt that the punishment for this crime is a fit case for the electric chair," Reid concluded, practically begging the judges to sentence Alex to death.

The first witness called was Absalom Moyer, who told the court that his daughter had left for school early on the morning of February 11, and he had not seen her again.

"When did you next see your daughter, Mr. Moyer?" Reid asked softly.

"In the morgue," Absalom whispered.

"Was she dead?"

"Yes." Helen's father answered, tears welling in his eyes.

Alex, nestled between his two attorneys, kept his eyes riveted to the table as Absalom testified. Those sitting close to him noticed, however, that throughout Mr. Moyer's testimony, the defendant clenched and unclenched his fists until the knuckles actually went white.

Next came a parade of lawmen—detectives, state troopers and local police—each testifying that Meyer had answered all of their questions willingly and in a cool and detached manner. No, the men said, he had never shown remorse for his crime.

Assistant District Attorney Philip Reilly then read Meyer's confession, telling the judges that only one change had been made to it. Originally, Meyer had said he was about 30 feet from Helen when he first saw he, but later requested that be changed to "35 to 40 feet."

By noon, the prosecution had rested, and MacElree rose to call his first witness: O. Jackson Meyer.

Alex's father looked like a crushed man as he walked stiffly to the witness stand. The strain of his son's ordeal was evident on his face, which appeared to have aged ten years in the last two months.

O. Jackson testified that his son was a good boy, but one with "problems." "He didn't feel pain," O. Jackson said, and "appeared immune to it."

Asked to explain, Alex's father gave an example. Several years ago Alex had been severely burned on the legs when a dynamite cap exploded. "I knew from my experience that the best thing to do was to clean out the burns, so I took a brush and hot water and scrubbed his legs hard. My son didn't scream or shed a tear. He didn't even complain." Another time, O. Jackson continued, Alex had been thrown from a moving vehicle and tossed more than 15 feet in the air. Despite the fact that he had sustained cuts and bruises, along with a huge knot on the back of his head, the boy hadn't appeared to feel any of these injuries.

There were other instances when his son should have howled with pain but remained mute. There were accidents around the house and on the farm, including falls, cuts, and several mishaps with animals: cows that had both kicked Alex and stepped on his toes, and at least two dog bites.

Many of those in the gallery had no idea how this testimony was supposed to help the defendant. Was it meant to show that if Alex didn't feel pain he wouldn't know his victim did either? Several others didn't believe the testimony at all, especially two former guards from Huntingdon who sat in the first row. These two men had worked at the reformatory when Alex was serving time there, and each remembered an occasion when he had been beaten up by his cellmate. At that time, they had found Alexander Meyer huddled in his cell "whimpering like a baby."

Besides O. Jackson, most of MacElree's remaining witnesses were doctors, beginning with Doctor William Drayton. Drayton had examined Alex when he first arrived at Huntingdon after his attack on Anna Blasch and Viola Bauder. He claimed that Meyer had the mentality and responsibility of a thirteen-year-old boy. "He had no thought, or fears as to the consequences of his actions," Drayton testified, "and was definitely retarded."

"What would you consider his propensity to commit future crimes?" MacElree asked.

Drayton admitted that Meyer was likely to re-offend. "The condition is inborn," he said sadly, "there is no chance of changing it."

Had Drayton favored paroling Alex? MacElree asked.

"I did not." Drayton answered. "I believed the boy had criminal tendencies and should not have been released."

Assistant District Attorney Joseph McKeone asked the doctor only one question on cross examination: "Was Alexander Meyer unable to help himself when he killed?"

"Mr. Meyer had it within himself to curb his desires on the day he ran down Helen Moyer," Drayton said firmly.

Doctor Arthur Philips, a psychologist employed at Huntingdon, was the next witness called by the defense. Philips described Meyer as having "infantile emotional reactions," and said he "suffered from an organic inferiority which led him to sadistic impulses and behavior."

"Did you favor the parole of this boy?" MacElree asked.

"Yes, sir."

"Even though Doctor Drayton said he had criminal tendencies and protested a parole?"

"Yes, sir."

"Will you tell the court why you approved?"

"Mr. Meyer had shown improvement in his work," Philips said simply.

"What kind of work?"

"Manual."

"How about his moral character?" MacElree challenged.

Philips hesitated for a moment before answering, "We felt he had improved physically, mentally, and of course, morally."

"Your Honors," District Attorney Reid suddenly interrupted, raising his hands in a helpless gesture, "I'm going to have to object."

Judge Windle, as if expecting the objection, nodded his head and waved his hand at Reid, indicating he should sit down. Then, turning to the defense attorney, the judge asked, "Where is this line of questioning going Mr. MacElree?"

Despite his look of innocence, MacElree knew exactly what he was doing. His strategy was to shift Meyer's guilt—or at least part of it—elsewhere, specifically, to the Commonwealth of Pennsylvania. "Your Honor," the attorney now said, "I'm trying to show that this boy never should have been paroled. This is a serious case and I owe a debt to the community. His parole was not fair, either to the community or to himself."

Windle hesitated for a moment before finally nodding his head, indicating that he would allow the questioning to continue.

"Doctor," MacElree resumed, turning back to his witness, "will you tell me, as man to man, whether, in your own conscience, Alexander Meyer was a fit subject to be at large?"

"In my opinion, yes," The doctor answered.

"Was Meyer discharged with no questions as to what would follow his release?"

"Certainly not." Philips replied, a bit huffily.

"Isn't it a fact," MacElree now asked, "that Alexander Meyer was paroled because of the policy of that institution—Huntingdon—that a certain number of boys be released due to overcrowding?"

"I'm not able to make that statement."

MacElree raised his eyebrows. "Well, can you contradict it?"

"No," Philips admitted softly. But he quickly protested that Meyer was not "discharged." "He was paroled with supervision."

MacElree's next witness caused a murmur to race through the courtroom. "Call Alexander Meyer."

Meyer, dressed in a dark suit and looking about thirty pounds lighter than when arrested, walked to the stand in a calm, cool manner and took a seat.

MacElree's tone was soft and comforting. "Alex, how old were you on February 11, 1937?"

"Nineteen."

"Nineteen," MacElree repeated, as if to imply that the defendant was a mere child. "And why did you kill Helen Moyer?"

"I didn't mean to kill her," Alex insisted, "I only wanted to clip her with the truck and knock her unconscious so I could attack her. But the truck slipped off of the pavement onto the shoulder of the road, and I hit her harder than I meant to."

MacElree seemed to blanch at the boy's answer, but quickly moved on. "And then you drove her ten miles to the abandoned farmhouse?"

"Yes," Alex said, offering no additional details; nor, for that matter, did his attorney ask for any. Skipping completely over the rape and disposal of Helen's body, MacElree now asked Alex why he felt he needed to "clip her with his truck."

Alex seemed to think about that, appearing perplexed by the question himself. Finally, he replied, "My mind wanders when I'm alone. When I'm working though, I get interested in my work."

Meyer's confession had already been read to the court, and District Attorney Reid, too, didn't feel he needed to elaborate on the details of Helen's rape and disposal. Instead, the district attorney asked about the other girls Alex had tried to lure into his truck.

Meyer didn't deny offering the girls a ride, but he hedged greatly on what his motive was in doing so. After several unsuccessful attempts to get him to admit that he intended to rape those "potential victims," Reid finally changed direction. "You said that you killed Helen because when you're alone your mind wanders, but when you're working you get interested in your work."

Alex nodded.

"Well, weren't you working on February 11, 1937?"

Again, Alex nodded. "I wasn't interested in the work I was doing that day, and the thought of girls always came into my mind at such times."

Alex had done absolutely nothing to help his own case. He came off as an arrogant, cold, and calculating killer. It was difficult to put your finger on what exactly it was, but Alexander Meyer was a strange individual. His words were somehow disconnected from what he was actually saying, and he appeared to lack any real emotion. One spectator would describe him in a manner which seemed fitting. "He was like a fish flopping around on the bed of your boat. He's cold and slimy and staring up at you with those dead eyes, and even though you know he's about to die, it's hard to feel sorry for him."

MacElree's last two witnesses were psychiatrists who had examined Meyer after his arrest for Helen's murder. Doctor A. M. Orenstein and Doctor Baldwin L. Keyes, both from Philadelphia, had each been paid $600 for their testimony. Orenstein, Assistant Professor of Neurology at the University of Pennsylvania, had examined Meyer in his jail cell, and concurred with earlier testimony that the boy was far below his age in mentality. But, Orenstein also testified, Meyer was cunning in his depravity, having told the psychiatrist; "If I had just held my tongue, they never would have been able to prove anything against me in court."

Reid asked only one rhetorical question of the doctor. "That's pretty intelligent reasoning for someone who's mentally retarded isn't it?"

After Keyes testified that he, too, concurred with earlier testimony as to Alex's mental deficiency, MacElree rested his case. Judges Windle and Harvey then adjourned court until the next morning.

Back in his jail cell, Meyer ate a late lunch and then chatted with a few reporters. He had no interest in discussing the proceedings which had just concluded, but instead began talking about having worked in West Virginia as a coal miner. "I love the south. It's wonderful country down there. Someday I'd like to live down there."

Uncomfortable hearing Alex talk about a future none of the reporters thought he'd live to see, one of them decided to change the subject by asking about his middle name.

"Thweatt. That's an unusual name. Where did it come from?"

Alex immediately brightened. "That was my grandfather's name on my mother's side," he said proudly. "My Grandpa was a civil war veteran and boy, could he tell a story!"

Soon, the press was ordered away and Alex went back to his bunk where he made himself comfortable and then smoked his traditional after-meal cigar.

The next morning, everyone once again assembled in Judge Windle and Harvey's courtroom in anticipation of closing arguments. MacElree argued passionately that but for Alex having been released from the Huntingdon Reformatory, this crime would never have happened.

"A death sentence would not correct the failure and negligence of the Commonwealth to see that Meyer was not at large," MacElree said with conviction. "Can the Commonwealth, in light of the testimony, escape its share of the responsibility in this case?"

Turning to look at his client, MacElree continued. "I want it fully understood that I am not asking for sympathy for Meyer. He is not entitled to it. I ask no pity for him. He does not deserve it."

At these words, Alex dropped his gaze to the table top, and his attorney turned back to address the judges.

"The State, at large, cannot ignore the bold challenge this case presents. If the death of Alexander Meyer answers that challenge, then by all means, send him to the chair. But if not, then consider the consent and approval of authorities from which he was released from an institution, after less than two years, and was again at large as a menace to society and himself. Helen Moyer should not have died," MacElree concluded softly, "because Alexander Meyer should not have been at large."

Helen's parents were in the courtroom, and as Assistant District Attorney Joseph McKeone rose to give the states closing argument, Absalom suddenly leaned forward in his seat, elbows resting on his knees, and stared intently at his daughter's killer. Alex caught the man's eyes and immediately lowered his head, staring at the table.

"If Alexander Meyer is given a life sentence," McKeone began, "there is always the possibility of escape, or pardon, or even murder within the prison walls. Mr. MacElree insists that if he had spent his maximum time in Huntingdon, this trial would never have occurred. We submit to you, however, that had Meyer spent his maximum time in Huntingdon, this trial would only have been delayed until a later date."

McKeone went on to describe Meyer as a cold-blooded and cunning murderer who knew exactly what he was doing. He urged Windle and Harvey to do the right thing by sentencing Alex to the electric chair. It was, he said, the only way they could ensure protection to girls and society at large.

Court was then dismissed, and everyone was ordered to reconvene at 10:00 am, on Monday, April 12, 1937, at which time sentence would be handed down. The fate of Alexander Meyer rested solely with two men: Judge Butler Windle and Judge Ernest Harvey.

~*~*~

The week passed slowly. Alex's family visited him often, as did his attorneys, and all of them were absolute wrecks emotionally. Everyone thought MacElree had done an excellent job in his closing, but they all knew that the chances of Alex avoiding the death penalty were slim to none. The crime was simply too heinous, the public's sentiment towards the killer too strong, and Alex's prior criminal record too severe.

The only person who didn't believe Alex would die for his crime was Alex himself. He remained convinced that he would beat the odds and be sentenced to prison rather than death, and he continued with his calm and unconcerned attitude throughout the entire week.

On Sunday, April 11, the day before sentencing, Louise Meyer visited Alex in his jail cell. Despite the fact that Louise was terrified for her son, Alex remained nonchalant about his predicament. Upset, Louise fled the jail in tears.

On the morning of Monday, April 12, Alex was woken early, his guards hoping to get him to court before the expected crowds arrived. He seemed in good spirits as he ate his usual breakfast and then lit his cigar, eager to chat with the guards. He talked once again about coal mining, and then turned the conversation to guns, telling in great detail how to take a weapon apart.

Although none of the guards were too fond of Alex, it was unsettling to be talking to a man who would probably be dead in only a few short weeks—not killed by illness or accident, but by murder itself.[2] Watching him chat casually about meaningless things caused one of his jailers to blurt out, "Aren't you afraid?"

Meyer paused in mid-sentence before answering. "I don't care what they do to me," he said coldly. "I'm not afraid to die." But each of the guards noticed that as he said those words, the hand that held his cigar began to tremble.

There was no one in the courtroom when Alex arrived, and he sat with his attorneys talking and joking as a few people began to enter the room. Soon, there was a steady stream of spectators flooding in, noisily taking their seats. Conspicuously absent, however, were any members of Helen's, family, or, for that matter, Alex's. Neither the Moyers nor the Meyers attended Alex's sentencing.

At precisely 10:00 am, Judges Windle and Harvey entered the courtroom and took their seats behind the bench. In all, the hearing lasted no more than five minutes.

"It is apparent," Windle began, reading from his opinion, "that the punishment to be visited upon one convicted of murder in the first degree is death, unless mitigating circumstances are present which render appropriate the lesser penalty of life imprisonment."

---

[2] Despite how people might view executions, the willful taking of a human life is defined as murder. Alexander Meyer's death, as well as all those executed by the state, would list homicide as the manner of death.

"That Alexander Meyer is a habitual offender against organized society cannot be doubted," Windle continued, "He is not customarily of law-abiding nature and habits. The medical experts all described him as anti-social. The psychologists at Huntingdon termed him a sadist. He has definite criminal tendencies. He does not learn by experience, and it is possible that he will commit crimes—and sex crimes—again."

At the defense table, MacElree felt his heart sink.

"To permit a man of dangerous criminal tendencies," Windle continued, "to be in a position where he can give indulgence to such propensities, would be folly which no community should suffer itself to commit, any more than it should allow a wild animal to range at will in the streets. If, therefore, there is danger that a defendant may again commit crime, society should restrain his liberty until such danger is past. And, in cases similar to the present—if reasonably necessary for the purpose—to terminate his life. Therefore, we are entirely satisfied that our decision is proper."

Windle leveled his gaze directly upon Alexander Meyer.

"After due consideration of the fact," he said, "and weighing the evidence, it is the opinion of this court that you shall suffer death in the electric chair, having pled guilty to a charge of first degree murder."

At that point, MacElree stood and motioned that Alex should join him. Visibly trembling, the youth walked with his attorney and stood before the bench.

"Alexander Meyer," the judge said, "you will be taken to Rockview Penitentiary at Bellefonte, Pennsylvania, to suffer death in the electric chair at a date to be set at a later time by the governor of this state, George H. Earle."

Asked if he had anything to say, Alex shook his head.

"Then may God have mercy on your soul."

The condemned prisoner, now escorted by six guards, was led out a back door, where a throng of highway patrolmen, local police, and special deputies, assigned to guard the courthouse, waited. Before being placed in the car, Alex caught sight of Assistant District Attorney Joseph McKeone, and stopped briefly to speak to him.

"I'm satisfied with the sentence," Alex said to the surprised prosecutor. "I just want to get it over with. The quicker the better." Then, with his guards urging him forward, the convicted killer was led back to the Chester County Jail to await his transfer to Rockview.

Members of the press made a mad dash for the Moyer house, where they found Helen's mother hanging out a load of wash in her backyard. When told of the death sentence, Melba paused for a moment, saying nothing. Then she began to cry.

"You know Helen's dream had been to be a missionary. I think the law has taken its course, but it doesn't bring back my daughter." Then, referring to Helen's killer, Melba dried her tears and her voice took on a confused tone. "He doesn't appear to be a bad sort of boy," she said. "I saw him the other day; he's not a bad-looking boy and he was dressed quite neatly." She shook her head, perplexed, then quickly dismissed him. "But my Helen was a good girl and she must have suffered a lot. I don't want anyone else to suffer, but I can never forget all this."

Paul MacElree, who was depressed that his argument hadn't worked, but also relieved to be done with the case, gave his own statement to the press. "I have no intention of contesting the judge's decision to the high courts," the attorney said, turning away from the cameras.

"You mean you won't appeal the sentence?" one of the reporters called out, surprised.

"I won't," MacElree answered as he hurried through the crowd.

~*~*~

Most people were thrilled with Alexander Meyer's death sentence, as indicated by the *8,000* requests the warden of Rockview Penitentiary received from people wanting to view his execution. There were, however, numerous anti-death-penalty people at the time, and the fact that Paul MacElree was not going to fight for his client's life upset them greatly.

On May 25, 1937, two Meadville, Pennsylvania attorneys, Albert Thomas and Fred Klebort, filed a petition with the parole board asking that they commute Meyer's sentence to life imprisonment.

Thomas argued that the convicted killer was "a sub-normal individual who acted under an irresistible impulse. He was totally unable to appreciate the consequences of his act." According to him, Alex's "irresistible impulse" was his sex drive. Meyer was still "mentally deficient and unable to realize the consequences of his illegal acts," Thomas said. "He would have to commit the crime of murder, not out of any design or intent, but more in the nature of an accidental result following his uncontrollable will (desire for sex)."

The Parole Board agreed to take the matter under advisement until their June session which would meet on June 17. Meanwhile, Governor George Earle set Alex's execution date for July 12, 1937.

It seemed only then that Alex finally realized that he was going to die for his crime. What his family had been enduring for the past four months, he, too, began to experience. He had trouble sleeping or eating. He paced his cell constantly, his fists clenching and unclenching, his fingernails digging into the flesh of his palms until they bled. His weight continued to plummet, and he began to resemble little more than a walking skeleton. Alarmed by this drastic change, and desperate to save his boy's life, on June 8, O. Jackson hired Doctor A. P. Noyes of Norristown State Hospital, one of the most highly-respected psychiatrists in the state, to consult with jail officials and examine his son. Although Noyes agreed that Meyer was close to a nervous breakdown, he could not help the boy or his father. He found nothing in his examination of Alex that would warrant stopping his execution.

On June 17, Attorney Thomas was once again before the parole board to argue for clemency for Meyer. Also present at the hearing was A.D.A. Joseph McKeone, ready to argue against commuting Meyer's sentence.

"Alexander Meyer was infirm mentally from birth," Thomas pleaded with the board. "He is the victim of a constitutional psychopathic inferiority." His condition, the attorney said, was mostly due to his inability to form a relationship with the opposite sex. Meyer had never had a girlfriend, the attorney claimed, and was perfectly sane except when "confronted with the sex desire." This was made clear, Thomas said, by the fact that four psychiatrists concurred with that assessment.

Had not those same four psychiatrists also noted that Alexander Meyer knew right from wrong? The board now asked.

Reluctantly, Thomas agreed that they had, but argued that if Meyer was to die, then "the state should throw open the doors of all their institution and execute anyone deemed 'not normal.' But who should decide who's normal?" Thomas asked in a soft voice. "If the board doesn't save this boy from the chair, then I'll walk the last mile with him."

McKeone had little to say to the board, other than to remind them that all the medical testimony had agreed on one point: Alexander Meyer had the ability to restrain himself at the time he chose to kill Helen Moyer.

The board agreed and denied clemency for the prisoner

Alex heard of the parole board's decision from the prison grapevine, and appeared to take the news calmly. He had returned to his old ways: eating and sleeping well, smoking cigars, reading magazines, and listening to the radio. He was either in complete denial about his fate or had finally accepted it.

With the parole board's decision not to grant clemency, plans began being made to transfer Alex to Rockview. It was soon decided that Meyer would be moved on July 10, two days before his scheduled execution.

Not everyone, however, had given up on trying to save Alex's life. On July 2, the Pennsylvania Prison Society wrote the following letter to Governor George Earle, begging him to grant a re-hearing in the Meyer case:

Dear Governor Earle,

The Meyer case is so extreme in its abnormality that only its atrocity, and the consequent emotional reaction of the community, obscure the otherwise obvious fact: that his was the act of an irresponsible person.

It seems that society would be better served if this unfortunate youth, and others guilty of abnormal crimes, were projected to prolong observation and intensive study. In this way only, can society develop methods for early detection and preventive treatment, of those who may be potential criminals. Certainly society cannot hope to make progress in the treatment of those with abnormal tendencies, so long as it clings to the archaic legal definition of insanity. A re-hearing is an obligation, due not only to the boy and his parents, but to the public as well.

We ask that you consider the Meyer case from this standpoint and make it possible to have a re-hearing. The Pennsylvania Prison Society protests vigorously against the annihilation of this unfortunate individual without further consideration.

A.G. Fraser, Executive Secretary

Not anticipating the Governor to interfere—which he didn't—plans for Meyer's execution continued. On July 8, Doctor L.U. Zech, the York County coroner was asked to assist Doctor H.S. Schwartz, prison physician at Rockview, in Meyer's autopsy after his execution. By law, the coroner was one of the few people required to witness the electrocution. Despite the thousands of requests received, Meyer's execution would be limited to a total of twelve people excluding prison personnel and the coroner: six witnesses and six members of the press.

On July 9, O. Jackson made a personal plea for his son's life to Governor George Earle. Earle, however, refused to interfere with Alex's death sentence. That same afternoon, Louise Meyer, with her daughter, visited Alex in his cell as officials in Harrisburg set the time of her son's execution for 1:30 am on July 12, 1937.

The next day, July 10, Alex, dressed in a brown suit and manacled to a Pennsylvania State Trooper, was taken from the Chester County Jail to Rockview State Penitentiary. Before leaving, he had asked Warden Musser to deliver a message to his father. "Tell my dad I want to be cremated, and my ashes scattered to the four winds."

Sheriff Fred Wahl, several state troopers, and Alexander Meyer arrived at Rockview around 3:10 pm on the beautiful Saturday afternoon of July 10, 1937. Sheriff Wahl shook Alex's hand and wished him luck before leaving, and then the doomed prisoner was taken directly to Rockview's death row.

Warden Ashe greeted his new prisoner and escorted him to his tiny cell where Alex made no requests and spent a normal night. The next day, Sunday, July 11, Alex spent most of the afternoon with the prison chaplain, C. F. Lauer, who was surprised by the youth's stoic calm. "He showed nothing unusual in temperament," Lauer later told the press, "and had no special requests."

In fact, Alex didn't even care about the traditional "last meal." When asked what he wanted, the prisoner simply shook his head. He would eat whatever the jail was serving, he said.

At 6:00 pm, guards brought his dinner to his cell: roast beef, mashed potatoes, stewed tomatoes, drop cakes, apple pie, iced tea and sugar. Alex sat on his cot eating quietly and gazing off into space, seemingly lost in thought. Shortly after he finished, the prison barber came in to shave the youth's head and left leg.

Executioner Robert Elliot, who served not only the state of Pennsylvania, but also New York, New Jersey, Vermont and Massachusetts, arrived around 10:00 pm, and went directly to the electrocution room. Elliot had been the states executioner since 1926, and had an impressive list of people whom he had put to death, including Richard Bruno Hauptmann, who was convicted of the Lindbergh baby kidnapping, Sacco and Vanzetti, two Italians convicted—but possibly innocent[3]—of murdering two men in Braintree Massachusetts, and Ruth Snyder, "the Granite Woman," who, with her lover Judd Gray, had murdered her husband in Queens, New York in 1927.

It was Elliot's habit to test the electric chair before the condemned prisoner came in. He first attached a board lined with small bulbs to the chair's electrodes, and then laid the board across the arms of the chair. Then, disappearing behind a long curtain, Elliot flipped a switch and the bulbs instantly lit up, indicating that there was electricity running to the chair. After removing the board, Elliot then soaked the small sponge that would line the helmet to be placed on Meyer's head. Meanwhile, guards busied themselves stringing rope around the room, separating the witnesses' section from the chair itself.

Those who were scheduled to watch the execution began arriving shortly before midnight and were escorted into Warden Ashe's office, located a short distance outside the prison gate. Deputy Warden C. C. Rhoades checked off each arriving guests name as they entered the room. At 1:05 am, Ashe indicated it was time to go, and everyone moved solemnly out the office door. It was a beautiful, clear night, the brightly shining starts illuminating a path from the office to the prison gate.

---

[3] In 1977, Massachusetts Governor Michael Dukakis proclaimed that Sacco and Vanzetti had been unfairly tried and convicted, and that "any disgrace should be removed forever from their names."

The electrocution building was a square, squat structure, and once inside, a guard unlocked a door and led the witnesses up a spiral staircase to the second floor. Arriving at a long hall, with the execution chamber all the way at the other end directly facing them, the witnesses were surprised, and somewhat uncomfortable, to realize they were now walking down Rockview's Death Row. They passed right in front of Alexander Meyer's cell and saw the youth sitting with Chaplain Lauer. The witnesses averted their eyes from the boy, embarrassed, and Meyer bowed his head as they walked by.

The actual execution room was a cold, stark place that seemed almost sterile in its simplicity. The walls were bare other than for a few signs which gave a one word warning: SILENCE. There were no chairs for the spectators, only two benches, one on each wall at opposite ends of the room. The electric chair itself sat glaringly alone in the middle of the room between the two benches. Upon entering, guards separated the witnesses into two groups; those there simply to witness the execution were directed to the left of the chair, while members of the press to the bench on the right.

Suddenly, the door the witnesses had just entered swung open with a bang and in walked Chaplain Lauer, reading softly from his Bible. Immediately following him, flanked by two guards, was Alexander Meyer. Helen Moyer's killer was no longer the cocky and arrogant youngster who had been arrested four months earlier, but a visibly trembling boy, who stopped short when confronted with the electric chair. He was dressed in a white shirt, which was opened halfway down his chest, and blue slacks, the left leg slit to above his knee. On his feet he wore gray socks and bedroom slippers.

After a moment, Alex regained his composure and walked stiffly to the electric chair, pausing only briefly before sitting down. The executioner, Robert Elliot, assisted by several guards, applied the electrodes and straps as Meyer glanced furtively around the room, once again nervously clenching and unclenching his fists. When Elliot finally placed the helmet on the condemned man's head, Alex visibly flinched, and then the death mask was lowered over his face and those watching saw him no more.

Quickly, Elliot disappeared around the curtain and flipped the switch, sending a current of 2,000 volts of electricity coursing through Alexander Meyer's body. The time was 1:32 am. As Elliot reduced the current, and then increased it again, Meyer's body jerked forward in the chair, straining against the straps, and then fell back again, only to leap forward once more when the executioner again increased the voltage.

Soon, the witnesses began to see smoke curling up from the boy's left leg, and then a thin wisp which wafted up from his covered head. His hands and arms—indeed all the skin that was visibly showing—soon took on a bizarre reddish tint. At 1:35 am, three minutes after he had first pulled the switch, Robert Elliot cut the power to the chair.

Doctor Schwartz, the prison physician, placed his stethoscope on Alexander Meyer's chest, listened for a moment, and then turned towards the members of the press. "Gentlemen," the doctor said loudly, "I pronounce Alexander Meyer dead."

Almost immediately, those who had viewed the execution were ushered out the door, walking so close to the body of Alex Meyer, still strapped in the electric chair, that they could have easily reached out and touched him. They had been in the execution building a mere 35 minutes, and the stars had been shining brightly when they entered. Now, however, they walked from the building into a torrential downpour. For some, who had never seen the State take a man's life before—and hoped to God they never had to witness such a thing again—the weather seemed almost fitting.

~*~*~

Alex's body was immediately taken to the prison morgue where Doctor's Schwartz and Zech, along with Zech's son, York County Deputy Coroner L. Edward Zech, conducted an autopsy.

The Meyer family had made arrangements with a local funeral director, Leland Wilson, to bring Alex's body back to Chester County. Notified that Meyer's autopsy was complete, Wilson, driving a black hearse, left his funeral home to travel to Bellefonte at 3:00 am, on July 13, 1937, arriving there at 7:00 am. Prison official's released Alex's body to him at 9:00 am.

On his return home, Wilson grimaced when he saw the crowd of reporters waiting for him. Word had leaked out that Alex had requested his body be cremated, and as soon as the funeral director exited the car he was surrounded by the press who asked if it were true. Raising his hands to hush them, Wilson said simply, "The family is still undecided about funeral plans."

It was true that O. Jackson and Louise had not yet decided what to do with Alex's remains. Although they knew of their son's wishes, the family owned a plot in Fairview Cemetery at Glenmoore and would have preferred to have him interred there. Wilson, although sympathetic to the family's plight, urged them not to delay the funeral, reminding them that to do so would only be feeding into the "morbidly curious."

In the end, O. Jackson and Louise honored their son's last wish. The body of Alexander Meyer was cremated on July 14, 1937. The boy had asked his father to "scatter his ashes to the four winds," but it is not known if O. Jackson honored this request or not. The Meyer family has never revealed what became of Alex's remains.

Postscript:

It was reported that Helen's family brought a $50,000 lawsuit against the Meyer's, charging them with negligence, and arguing that since O. Jackson and Louise knew of their son's mental condition, they should not have allowed him the freedom to do as he pleased. What became of the lawsuit, however, is unknown.

Robert Elliot, the man who executed Alexander Meyer, was paid $150.00 for the job, plus traveling expenses. He died in 1939, after having put some 378 people to death.

Many newspapers reported that Alex Meyer attacked Jennie Watterson when she refused to get into his truck. Meyer, however, in his confession, said that Jennie did get into his truck, and I chose to write the event in that way. I did this because I felt that scenario best fit the evidence. It would have been difficult for Meyer to attack the girl with a screwdriver if she were outside the truck and him in. Although it's unknown what became of the other girls Alex tried to lure into his truck, it is known that Jennie Watterson went on to marry and have a family of her own before passing away several years ago.

As far as can be determined, the murder of the unidentified woman found near the Meyer farm five years before Alex murdered Helen has never been solved.

The $1,000 reward offered in the case was split evenly among William Crawford, the scrap worker who actually witnessed Meyer hit Helen, and William Parry and his daughter, who reported seeing Alex's truck with the broken headlight in Glenmoore.

Someone was eventually tried and convicted for the murder of Mary Ellen Babcock, the young girl from Buffalo, New York, whose death police initially thought Meyer might have been involved in.

The murder of Helen Moyer was a tragic and senseless crime, and the police work used to solve it was a fine example of patience, gumption, and diligent investigating. I have little doubt that Alexander Meyer would have continued to kill, and in all likelihood would have become a serial killer had his career not been stopped when it began.

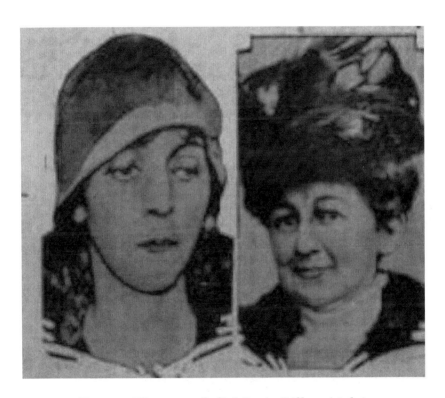
Frances Thomsen, (left) Minnie Dilley, (right).

Carl Thomsen

Alexander Meyer, (right), handcuffed to County Detective Francis Grubb

Crowds gather outside the old Guthrie place

Police guarding Helen's body after it was recovered from the well

The West Chester Jail, where Alexander Meyer was held

Alexander Meyer and his victim, Helen Moyer, (inset)

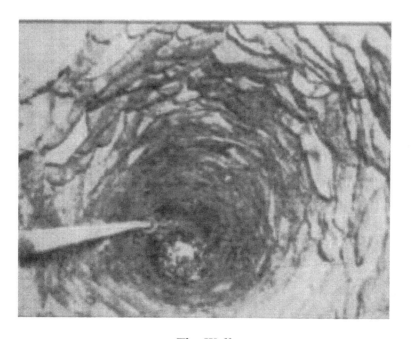

The Well

Albert Shinsky lies on his jail bunk reading True Confessions

Officer points at window through which Susan Mummey was shot

Selena Bernstel holding a black cat

Susan Mummey's house.

Rose McCloskey

Annie and Patrick McCloskey at the funeral of their daughter Rose

MISSING PERSON

Harriet Keim – Missing from home since 6 AM on 9/30/2014, Herrick Center, Pa. 18430.

Caucasion, age 84, 5'1", 100 lbs, slight build, pale complexion, green eyes, grey/silver shoulder length hair. Last seen wearing embroidery flower on front of carmel shirt, loafers with blue tassel, jeans, and a purse.

If sighted or **any** other information:

Please call the **PA State Police** @ **570-465-3154** or **911**

http://www.facebook.com/helpfindharrietkeim

THE HEX SLAYER

(Pottsville, PA The murder of reputed 'witch' Susan Mummey.)

INTRODUCTION

Magic, sorcery, witchcraft and the occult; four words that immediately conjure up images of spells and cauldrons and the infamous Salem witch trials of the early 1600s. Some people might be surprised to know that Massachusetts was not the only state to have a history with the supernatural; Pennsylvania had its own brush with such panic and lunacy as well. Even today, when one drives through the southwestern portion of the state—through the rolling green hills of what's come to be known as Dutch Country—one can still see the strange symbols that adorn the picture-perfect barns and well maintained farmhouses. Colorful hand-painted signs that depict a multitude of images: horses, birds, flowers and stars.

Most people pay little attention to these signs anymore, viewing them merely as a tradition or a decoration, while others have no idea *what* they are or why they're there. The old timers know of course—know all too well the power of the hex and the need to guard against it with a "hex sign"—and many of them wouldn't risk spending the night in a building that wasn't protected by one.

Originating in the dark forests of Europe, during the middle-ages, the belief in the hex was brought to this country by early settlers of German descent. These were people who believed that some were endowed with the power to cast spells, turn the evil-eye, or put a hex (curse) on you. Such curses could result in illness and tragedy that might plague a victim for the rest of their life unless the spell was broken.

Of course, if one were endowed with the power to curse, then surely others were endowed with the power to heal, and soon the pow-wow[4] doctor was born. Both men and women, claiming the ability to thwart such spells and curses, quickly took up the practice of folk magic. They brewed strange concoctions for their patients, gave them odd amulets to wear, and provided them with eerie chants to repeat and bizarre practices to keep, all in an effort to end the suffering of those put under the hex. Strange symbols were also affixed to houses and barns; magical charms that would ward off and prevent the unholy spells that might otherwise be cast.

Such beliefs and practices arrived in America—and Pennsylvania—more than 200 years ago, and continued unchecked for decades, automatically being passed down from generation to generation. Over time, however, with the study and eventual acceptance of both science and education, these superstitious beliefs in curses and spells slowly began to fade. Such practices—at one time firmly believed in and looked upon with fear and dread—were now considered a form of mental illness. Indeed, by the early 1900s, one would have been hard pressed to find anyone who admitted to a belief in them, most claiming that that sort of thing went out ages ago, right along with vampires, werewolves, and the like.

For many, perhaps it had, but in the back mountains of Pennsylvania, in the true heart of Dutch Country, the beliefs persisted; often with deadly results

---

[4]Not to be confused with the Native American Pow-wow. The Pow-Wow Doctoring referred to in this story is a brand of faith healing using charms and magic, and has no direct connection to the Indian pow-wow or folk medicine.

"Thou shalt not suffer a witch to live."

March 17, 1934 was a blustery cold day; the kind of day that reminded residents of the small town of Ringtown, Pennsylvania—located in Schuylkill County, 17 miles southwest of the city of Hazelton—that winter was far from over. Ringtown consisted mainly of farmers and farmland, and even in 1934 living conditions there would have been described as somewhat primitive. Indeed, few of the town's inhabitants had either electricity or indoor plumbing, and a telephone was a luxury virtually unheard of.

One of the residents living there at the time, in the mountainous hills just outside of town, was sixty-three-year-old Susannah Furhman Mummey. Susannah, or Susan, as she was called, had been born on July 29, 1870, the youngest of four children. In 1891, by the age of twenty-one, Susan had married to a man named Isaac Brown, and given birth to a daughter, Amy. The marriage apparently didn't last, however, because by 1904 she was married to Henry Mummey—a man who had four children by a previous marriage—and eventually would give birth to her second daughter, Tovillia[5]. By 1934, Susan was a widow with something of a reputation in the Ringtown area.

---

[5] Tovillia may not have been Susan's natural child. Some newspaper articles refer to her as Susan's step-daughter, others as her niece. She may have been either. Despite the fact that Tovillia called Susan Mummey her mother, her age was reported as being only twenty-years-old, which would mean she was born four years after Henry Mummey's death. Her age, however, may have been reported inaccurately.

Twenty-four years earlier, in the summer of 1910, Susan had a dream, or perhaps it was a feeling, or maybe even a vision, that if her husband went to work on a particular day, she would never see him again. Henry Mummey worked in the crushing department at the DuPont Powder Mill, a dangerous job that required crushing the powder to be used in explosives. Susan's feeling had greatly upset her, and she begged her husband not to go to work on July 5, 1910. Henry, however, had merely scoffed at her concerns. He had five children to support, he told her; he *had* to go to work.

That same afternoon, a violent explosion ripped through the DuPont Powder Mill, leveling the building and blowing Henry Mummey 50 feet into the air. He landed in the top of an apple tree, horribly burned, mangled, and soon dead.

Susan's eerie premonition became a local legend in the land, and from that day forward she was looked upon as having special powers. She was clairvoyant, people thought, a seer, a psychic, maybe even a witch. Many of the town folk avoided the old woman after that, and others became downright afraid of her.

Susan lived in an isolated location; in a ramshackle and dilapidated farmhouse tucked away in the hills two-and-a-half miles outside of Ringtown. She shared her home with her daughter, Tovillia, who was twenty-years-old, and, with a boarder by the name of Jacob Rice. Rice had a badly injured foot and was staying with Mummey so she could tend to the wound.[6]

That Saturday, March 17, 1934—St. Patrick's Day—had been a busy one for Susan. She was worried about her boarder's foot, which didn't seem to be healing properly, and had spent the day caring for him, Tovillia, and the few animals she still kept on the farm. The old woman was exhausted and eager to go to bed, but there was still work to be done. The dinner dishes were yet to be washed, the fire needed tending, and Jacob's wound dressing would need to be changed one last time before morning.

---

[6] Some reported that Susan was actually pow-wowwing Rice's injury.

Around 7:00 pm, with her other chores taken care of, Susan carried a lighted oil lamp to the living room and had her patient rest his foot upon the coffee table. The light was dim, the farmhouse drafty, and as she unwound the soiled bandage, the howling wind outside flickered the flame of the lamp, casting eerie shadows along the bare wooden walls. Susan called for Tovillia to bring a second lamp, and the young girl did, holding it near Jacob Rice's foot.

As Susan bent to take a closer look, she and her two companions were suddenly rocked by a thunderous roar that seemed to shake the house on its very foundation. Instantly, the living room window exploded in a hail of wood chips and glass, allowing a bitter wind to howl through and immediately extinguish both lamps. Susan slumped to the ground as Tovillia and Jacob, their ears ringing, began groping about in the terrifying dark. Neither of them had any idea what had just happened, until a second explosion roared through the room again. Then it was clear; the deafening noise had come from a shotgun. *My God*, each of them thought as they dropped to the floor and quickly took cover, *someone is trying to kill us.*

Tovillia began to scream and Jacob Rice lay on the floor with his arms covering his head. Suddenly, everything went quiet. Five minutes passed, and then ten, the eerie silence somehow more unnerving than the chaos that had preceded it. Finally, Jacob Rice, while still lying on his stomach, raised his head a few inches and looked around. It was pitch black in the farmhouse, and the man could see nothing. Gearing up his nerve, he raised himself a little farther, this time up on his elbows.

"Susan?" He whispered, terrified that the gunman was still there, ready to shoot at the sound of his voice.

"Susan," he repeated, slightly louder, but all Jacob Rice heard was a pitiful whimpering coming from the corner of the room.

"Toddy?" he asked, using Tovillia's nickname. "Toddy, are you okay?"

The whimpering grew louder, and Rice began crawling along the floor towards it, following the sound, trying to be as quiet as possible.

"Shhh," he whispered as he moved ever closer to the terrified girl, but Toddy only whimpered louder, seemingly unable to control her terror. When Rice finally reached her, the penetrating dark made it impossible for him to see, and he began groping at her, attempting to determine if she were injured or not.

"I'm okay," Tovillia sobbed, clinging desperately to the man, her hold so tight it was nearly suffocating. "Where's my mom?"

"I don't know," Jacob replied, turning back to look where he had previously been sitting. "*Susan!*" he called again, pulling away from the clinging Tovillia. "Let me go check on her Toddy," Rice said, trying to remove her arms from around his neck. But Toddy clung ever tighter, shaking her head, whimpering again.

"No," she cried, pulling him close. "Don't leave me here. He'll kill me."

Jacob Rice hesitated for a moment, and then settled down next to the hysterical girl, accepting that there was probably nothing he could do for Susan Mummey anyway. And there the two of them remained, the young, terrified girl and the injured man, huddled in the corner of the living room, cowering in the dark.

The night seemed to go on forever. The shattered window had left the two stunned victims shivering in the cold and terrified over what had happened. They listened for any sound from Susan, and called out to her several times, but they heard nothing, and never received a reply. At one point, Jacob Rice lit the lamp and held it near his landlord's slumped body, but Toddy, afraid that the killer was still lurking outside, immediately began begging him to extinguish the lamp, and Rice complied. He had seen enough as it was; Susan's eyes were open, fixed, and dilated, and he knew instinctively that she was dead.

When the gray light of dawn began to wash over the old farmhouse—revealing the carnage those left inside had miraculously survived—Jacob finally convinced Toddy that he had to go get help. Susan Mummey didn't have a phone, and although Jacob's wound made it difficult for him to walk, he was the only hope they had. Toddy was certainly in no condition to try and make the trip.

After checking outside, and assuring the dazed girl that the killer was nowhere in sight, Jacob Rice began his long walk to the nearest neighbor more than a mile away. As the injured man hobbled through the woods in the bitter cold, Toddy remained alone in the house, sitting near her mother's now cold corpse.

When Rice finally arrived at the neighbor's, he found that they too didn't have a telephone. When Jacob told them that Susan Mummey was "hurt bad," and begged them to get help, the neighbor drove Rice to a doctor's office in Ringtown, who in turn summoned the police.

County detectives Louis Buono and John Fearns were the first to arrive on the scene at the farmhouse. While trying to calm the hysterical Toddy, each man noted that Susan Mummey was lying face down on the living room floor, and appeared to have been shot once in the right side of the chest. Later, the medical examiner would determine that the bullet had passed through Susan's lung and heart, and then lodged in her stomach, killing her almost instantly.

As Buono surveyed the scene, he noticed a bullet hole in the living room wall, almost directly behind where Susan Mummey lay. Using a small pocketknife, Buono dug in the hole and extracted a lead slug, ¾ of an inch in diameter. The officer knew it was a hand-made bullet that would fit a 12-gauge shotgun. It was common ammunition in the area, the locals referring to it as a "pumpkin ball," or sometimes a "magic ball."

Back in Ringtown, the doctor who had first notified local authorities had also called the Pennsylvania State Police at Tamaqua, and shortly after Buono found the bullet they arrived at the scene and began questioning the dead woman's daughter. Toddy told the investigators that Susan had been threatened many times in the past and had had problems with several of their neighbors. Bluntly, she told the detectives that the murder had been an assassination.

Authorities tended to agree with her, although they were baffled as to what the old woman might have done to warrant a "hit" on her. Still, it seemed obvious that this wasn't just some stray bullet that had accidentally found a target. Whoever had killed Susan Mummey had stood right on her porch, aimed his gun through the window, and deliberately fired it. The bullet had hit the woman intentionally, of that police were sure, but who would want to kill her, and why?

Susan Mummey seemed an unlikely target for murder. She had few close friends, rarely left her farmhouse, and was involved in nothing. She was simply an aging widow, living out her days in the mountainous hills of Pennsylvania. Although several of the officers knew of Mummey's reputation as a witch, their theory of the crime had little to do with that.

Central Pennsylvania was like any other hill-country in the nation; a backwoods region where fights and disputes among neighbors were common. Just in the area of Ringtown alone, several of these feuds had found their way into the local court systems. To those working the Mummey investigation, the old woman's murder looked a lot like that.

"I'll bet it turns out to be nothing more than a hillbilly mountain feud between two families," one officer said laconically. "Probably over something trivial like land."

As things turned out, the officer was right. Well, sort of.

~*~*~

Word of the cold-blooded murder of Susan Mummey spread like wildfire through Ringtown and its adjacent areas. Violence—this type of violence—was rare in the hill country, and people were concerned that there was some lunatic running loose, shooting innocent strangers at random.

Police questioning locals quickly learned that Susan Mummey had made a whole slew of enemies in the region. It seemed she not only fought and bickered with everyone around, but the officers heard countless stories of the old woman's reputation as a witch as well. Susan had berated her neighbor for his cows trampling her corn, had turned an "evil eye" on her banker over a mortgage dispute, and had 'hexed' another neighbor's horse until it fell ill and died. It seemed there were several people who might have wanted to see Susan Mummey dead, but there was one name in particular repeatedly mentioned as the most likely suspect: John Stone.*

Stone was Mummey's nearest neighbor, and the two had had an ongoing feud over both property boundaries and who was responsible for mending the fences that separated their land. Several area residents told the officers that Stone had threatened Susan in the past, so Detectives Buono and Fearns decided to pay him a visit.

Arriving at Stone's house, the officers were amused, though not surprised, to see that the central groove around his front door was completely filled with quicksilver, a remedy commonly used for warding off "evil threats." Local authorities were well aware of the hysteria that dwelled within the area and the strong belief many residents had in witches, sorcerers, and the hex. Apparently, John Stone was one of them.

When Stone finally answered the door after repeated knocking, he refused to let the officers in. Buono knew Stone, and he was aware that the man had a 12-gauge shotgun capable of firing the "pumpkin ball" that had killed Susan Mummey. He asked Stone about it.

"Sure," Stone said casually, "I have a 12-gauge shotgun, just like everybody else in the area, but I didn't kill Susie."

When asked if they could see the weapon, Stone refused. Buono was becoming frustrated with the man—he was investigating a brutal murder, and had no time to play games—and angered by Stone's lack of cooperation, the detective immediately placed him under arrest.

Once at the police station, John Stone spoke more freely about Susan Mummey and his hatred for her. He admitted that the two of them had been feuding over minor issues for years, and claimed that Susan was a witch.

"She hexed my mules, so that they'd bolt and run at the sight of me," he said. He also admitted that he felt "relief" that the witch was dead, but again denied killing her.

Stone's shotgun had been confiscated, but it was soon established not to have been the weapon used to kill Susan Mummey. After 24 hours, with nothing to hold him on, Stone was released and officers continued with their investigation. But despite the fact that they questioned scores of people in the area, no one claimed to have any knowledge of the crime.

Three days passed, leaving authorities frustrated that they were still no closer to finding Susan Mummey's killer. Then, on March 21, they finally got the break they had been waiting for. Four youths approached Detective Buono to tell him of seeing a vehicle parked on the lane leading to the Mummey house around 6:00 pm Saturday night, March 17. No one had been around the vehicle, the boys said, and it didn't appear to be stuck or broken down. It was just sitting there, parked on the side on the road. Asked to describe it, one of the youths said confidently, "Well, it was Al Shinsky's jitney."

Buono felt a sinking sensation in the pit of his stomach on hearing the boy's words. He knew Shinsky, a young man who drove a taxi (jitney) for local mine workers. "Are you sure it was Al's jitney?" Buono asked.

"Sure I'm sure," the youth said. "No doubt about it."

Albert Shinsky was a native of Ringtown, and at the time of the Mummey murder, he was twenty-three-years-old, tall, handsome, and well-liked within his community. He came from a large family, had several siblings, well-respected parents, and a lovely fiancé by the name of Selena Bernstel.

Born on November 11, 1908, Albert was a good baby, who grew into an active little boy. He was well-mannered, a hard worker from an early age, and although not stupid, the boy was, never-the-less, woefully naive. Growing up in Pennsylvania Dutch Country, Al had heard all the tales of witches and sorcerers and those who could cast spells or give you the evil eye. While there were many who considered such stories nothing more than fantasy and folklore, Albert Shinsky was not one of them. He believed in the tales, and the power of the hex, more deeply than anyone ever realized, even his own family.

Upon completing his schooling, Al took a job as a farm-hand, doing hard manual labor from sun-up to dusk. At night, he would go out with friends, often not coming home until the wee hours of the morning, but he never seemed to have any trouble putting in a full day's work after only a few hours of sleep. Everyone would agree that Al Shinsky possessed a youth and vitality that most people envied.

Gradually, however, things began to change, although the changes were so subtle at first that those close to him barely seemed to notice. It all began when Al was seventeen and abruptly quit his job as a farm-hand, giving no explanation for his sudden departure. He took a job in a local coal mine but once again quit after only a brief period, citing a lack of energy to perform his tasks.

By this time, those close to Al weren't surprised with his excuse. They had long since noticed how lethargic and frail the boy had become. He seemed to no longer have any strength or vigor, and complained bitterly of always being weak and tired. Even his appearance had changed from that of a healthy young lad to that of a thin, haggard old man, appearing far older than his actual years. Gone, too, were the days when he would go out with his friends each evening. Now, other than to drag himself to work—a chore in itself—the boy rarely ventured out of the house. Indeed, so slow did Albert Shinsky's movements become, that those who knew him had sarcastically christened him with a new nickname: "Speed."

At one point, Al suddenly packed his bags and moved away, incredibly landing a most coveted job with the power company in New Jersey. It was work that paid well and wasn't too demanding, but after only a few weeks he arrived back at his parents' house offering no explanation for his return. Since then he had been working as a jitney driver for the local coal miners, a job that required very little physical exertion.

Nearly seven years had passed since Al Shinsky abruptly quit his job as a farm-hand and seemed to change almost overnight. There were those who thought him simply lazy, while others barely remembered a time when he was any different than he was right now. Sure, they would say, Al Shinsky was an odd duck, strange even, but harmless; the type of guy who wouldn't hurt a fly.

Now, however, both detective Buono and Fearns were being told that Al's jitney cab was seen on the lane leading to the Mummey house, right around the time of the murder. Shinsky would need to be questioned, and later that same evening, March 21, 1934, detective Buono drove over to his house to pick him up.

After Buono knocked on the door, Al's mother yelled upstairs for her son and then shut the door softly, leaving the detective to wait outside. After a few minutes, Buono was startled to see an upstairs window open, and Al Shinsky climb out. The youth jumped onto the roof of a nearby shed and then disappeared from sight as he slid off the back edge. Believing his suspect was attempting to flee, Buono made a dash towards the shed, and nearly collided with Al Shinsky as he walked casually around the corner of the building, grinning foolishly.

"What the hell were you doing?" Buono shouted in surprise.

Shinsky looked puzzled by the question, and then glanced up at his bedroom window. Shrugging, he told the officer that he always entered and left his room that way.

Buono shook his head in bewilderment, and then escorted his suspect back to police headquarters. He and Fearns brought the young man a bottle of pop and then took seats across the table from him. They stared at the youth for a moment before Buono finally began.

"Albert," he said softly, "we've had reports that your vehicle was seen on the lane leading to the Mummey residence the night Susan Mummey was killed. Were you out there that night?"

"I sure was," Albert answered easily.

"What were you doing out there?"

Shinsky hesitated for a moment before answering the detective's question, but he displayed no hint of worry or fear, only something akin to relief. "I went out there to kill Mrs. Mummey," he said.

Shocked by the admission, Buono blurted out, "Why?"

Al Shinsky took a deep breath, shifted to a more comfortable position in his chair, and then began to tell his story of the murder of Susan Mummey. It was a tale that detective Buono would find unbelievable, bizarre, even fantastic, but, unfortunately, not all that surprising.

~*~*~

Nearly seven years earlier, Albert told the detectives, when he was just seventeen-years-old, he had been working for a farmer who owned land adjacent to the Mummey farm. There had been a bitter dispute over property boundaries between his employer and Susan Mummey, a fight that seemed to drag on forever and threatened to continue throughout the foreseeable future.

Susan had claimed that a certain section of land was hers and allowed her cows to graze on it despite Albert's employer ordering her to get them off. Soon, the farmer had erected a fence to keep his neighbor's animals off the piece of land he claimed as his own. Susan Mummey was furious about the fence, which she believed was placed on her property.

One day, Albert continued, while he was cutting across the fenced pasture to go fishing, Susan Mummey had come to the fence and stared at him.

"She caught me with her eyes," Al said breathlessly, shuddering at the thought, "and I began to sweat—a cold sweat—and then I felt a pair of hands pushing down on my shoulders. It felt like someone had me by the throat and I began running around and around, trying to shake off its grip, but I couldn't do it." Shinsky's voice was getting louder and louder as he related his tale, the anxiety of the memory clearly evident.

"After that," he continued, "I went back to the house and couldn't work. Since then, I've been bewitched. She put the hex on me that day, and for seven years I've suffered physical and mental torment."

"Physical and mental torment how?" Buono asked.

Al claimed that after that day his strength had left him and he was forced to leave dances because he got "too weak." He had endured "indescribable tortures" while Mummey had him "hexed." He was unable to work, suffered from insomnia, and was ill, depressed, and tired. He had left his job on the farm immediately, and went to work in the coal mines, but "the spell made me too weak to work." He had even tried to leave the area, he admitted, hoping to break the hex by going to work in New Jersey, but the spell was still upon him, so he had to come back.

"When the hex overtook me," Shinsky said, wide-eyed and serious, "I would feel hands on my shoulders, pins sticking into my sides, and my heart would start to pound in my chest. Susie sent a black cat down from the skies to tear and claw at me while I slept; to claw and tear at my sides. The cat would grow so large that I was almost smothered in its fur. I couldn't kill it. I couldn't do anything. The cat would spit and snarl at me, and its eyes glowed red with fire. Sometimes its face changed, and it was the face of the witch, Susie Mummey."

Buono and Fearns were well aware of the locals' belief in witchcraft and the hex, but they had never before been face to face with it in such a serious investigation. They were stunned to see Albert Shinsky's reaction as he related the horrors he claimed to have suffered under Susie Mummey's hex; the boy was near tears, and actually beginning to hyperventilate.

"When the cat came, my body would go ice cold," Shinsky continued, leaning across the table towards his interrogators, trying to emphasize his point. "I couldn't work, and when my family asked why, and I tried to tell them, they didn't believe me. They said I was just too lazy to work."

Shinsky went on to tell the detectives that he could no longer climb the stairs to his bedroom because, "when I do, the cat leaps out at me." He turned to Buono, and explained that that was why he had climbed out his bedroom window and onto the shed roof. He had been doing so for years.

"Didn't you seek help for this?" Fearns asked suddenly, his look one of stunned disbelief.

"I did," Al admitted, nodding his head. "I went to physicians for help, and they told me to take cold showers for a nervous condition." He laughed bitterly, and then dropped his voice to a mere whisper. "I knew all the time you couldn't kill the Devil with cold water."

He had also gone to priests at different times, Al continued, searching in vain for some relief from the "witch's" spell, but they couldn't help him either. It was after that that he decided to go and see the pow-wow doctors. They had given him strange concoctions to drink, he said, including fireflies in a glass of water that had to be served to him by his "sweetheart," Selena Bernstel, and fresh milk from a cow before the moon left the sky.

This last statement brought a grin to Albert's face as he admitted that he had "gone up and down the valley waking up farmers before dawn in order to drink their cows' fresh milk."

The pow-wows had done other things as well: given him amulets to wear, insisted he sleep with a board under his mattress, and taught him a chant to repeat whenever the cat appeared. The chant had worked, but the cat always came back, and often Al was too paralyzed with fear to remember to say it.

Buono found himself feeling sorry for the lad, who he had no doubt believed every word he was saying. The young man explained that he had lived like this for the past seven years, brooding upon the witch's curse, and trying to find a way to break it. The answer had finally come, Albert said, when a spirit from the sky had descended upon him and urged him to kill Susie Mummey. Susie was in cahoots with the Devil, the spirit had said, and even though it (the spirit) had made him ill, it had also told him that killing Susie was the only way he could break the spell. He had gone to the Mummey farmhouse on several occasions, he now admitted, intent on killing the old woman, "but the spell had been too strong," he said sadly.

On the evening of March 17, however, Shinsky said he knew he could wait no longer. The spell would never be broken unless he shed the witch's blood. So, after borrowing a 12-gauge shotgun from a friend, and loading it with a "magic bullet,"—used to kill witches—he had gone to her house and shot her.

"How do you feel now?" Buono asked, his mind reeling from the bizarreness of the confession.

"Like a re-born man," Shinsky replied.

Detective Buono found himself shuddering at the smile gracing the young man's face. To him, it was a look of sheer ecstasy.

Albert Shinsky's tale of witches and spells and having the hex put on him made news around the country and shocked most everyone who read about it, with the exception of those living in the south-central part of Pennsylvania. In that section of the state, whether you believed in such things or not, it was impossible not to know about them. Incidents pertaining to magic and curses had been occurring there for decades.

Few people had forgotten about old John Dice, who had served time in prison for selling his gullible customers "sea-monster tears" said to ward off evil spirits. Dice had been convicted on a charge of practicing pow-wow, although the charge should have been fraud when it was learned that his sea-monster tears were nothing more than salt-water. Then there was Mary Galgadora, who was so convinced that witches had invaded her hometown, she began a campaign to exterminate them by trying to brand suspects with hot coals. Several women had their lives turned upside down when they were reported to the authorities as being witches, and parents who had lost children publicly blamed their deaths on spells that had been cast on them.

As comical as some of these incidents may have been, authorities knew that others were far more serious. Only a few years before, John Beard, a sixty-five-year-old farmer, convinced that someone was trying to cast a spell on him, had barricaded himself in his shed and shot at anyone who approached. And sometimes, just like the case of Albert Shinsky, the hysteria turned deadly.

On March 24, 1922, police were summoned to the home of Sallie Jane and Irvin Samuel Heagy, where they found Irvin shot to death in his bed, and Sally hysterical. Not only was the woman hysterical, but she was also violent to the point where the officers needed to strap her down on an ironing board until a doctor could arrive and give her a sedative. Sallie Jane was muttering over and over that she didn't want to kill her husband, but, "I was under the influence of a spell. I couldn't help it. Spirits were guiding my hand."

For the past five years, Sallie Heagy had been acting queerly. Convinced that someone had cast a spell on her, she began visiting witch doctors who quickly confirmed her suspicions. Sallie had paid one of these pow-wow doctors $10.00 to rid her home of the effects of the witches, and the doctor had written a letter that he instructed her to hang above her door to ward off the spirits. Sallie had done this, but the letter did no good, and the spirits were still there. After more visits the pow-wows eventually convinced Sallie that the spell could not be broken because he who had cast it lived in the same house as she.

Sallie and Irvin had no children, and upon realizing that it had to have been her own husband who had given her the evil-eye, Sallie fled to her sister's house, but Irvin soon showed up to fetch her back. On the ride home, Sallie threatened to kill her husband, and even attempted to blow the two of them up by dropping a lit match into the gas tank of the car. Irvin, not believing in magic or the hex, drove his wife to Harrisburg where he consulted with medical doctors to try and get her help. After examining her, the doctors told Irvin that his wife should be admitted to a mental hospital immediately. Irvin, however, was reluctant to do this and instead, drove Sallie back home and tried to deal with her mental instability himself. He did, however, take some precautions. He and Sallie's brother removed all the weapons from the home as well as the ammunition.

Unbeknown to either of them, Sallie had hidden one of their guns, a revolver, and two days before the murder she confronted her husband with it. A struggle ensued, and Irvin managed to wrestle the gun away from her which he then placed in a locked box, nailing the top shut for added security.

Finally accepting that the doctors were right—his wife needed major help—Irvin reluctantly acquiesced to their suggestion that she be admitted to a sanatorium. Ironically, the very day Sallie Heagy murdered her husband, she was scheduled to be admitted to the Mt. Hope Sanitarium just outside of Baltimore. But before dawn, Sallie Heagy crept out of bed, and using an axe, broke open the box and retrieved the revolver her husband had placed there. Then, using a shell she had also secreted away, she loaded the gun and shot her husband while he slept.

Now, Sallie Heagy was being driven to jail, instead of the hospital, where she would be charged with one count of murder. Sallie, however, would never stand trial for her crime. Instead, on April 6, 1922—less than two weeks after she had killed her husband—Sallie Heagy was found hanging in her jail cell, having taken bed clothing from her bunk, fashioned it into a noose and tied it to a cross bar on her window.

A more recent case was that of twenty-two-year-old Verna Delp, who was found dead in a field near Catasauqua on March 15, 1929. Verna's father had long been a patient of pow-wow doctors, and when Verna herself fell ill, and traditional medical attention didn't help, her father sent her to the pow-wow doctors as well. The witch doctors pow-wowed the girl, and Verna began to get better. In fact, when she left home on the morning of Friday, March 14, it was to go see one of these doctors, Carl T. Bloom.*

The next day, Verna's body was found near a shed on the grounds of the Catasauqua gun club. It had rained hard on the night of March 14, but Verna's clothing was dry, and despite the fact that the grounds were muddy, her shoes and dress were clean. The body was laid out as if for burial, with Verna's hands crossed upon her chest, and there were no visible signs of injury on the girl. But pinned to her dress, directly over her heart, were two cryptic notes bearing mystic pow-wow symbols. The first note contained the letters N.I.R. in the form of a cross, followed by, *"Sanctus Spirits—all this he guarded here in time and there in eternity—amen,"* followed by three crosses. The second read *"Christ in the midst of peace went with his disciples ahead—St. Matthew, St. John, St. Luke, St. Mark—the four evangelists protect me Verna Octavia Delp by the ever praised Majesty and Unity of God. J.J.J. amen I. C. V. J. I. 3. 121. be with me at all destiny (three crosses) amen."*

At her autopsy, police made a startling discovery; not only were traces of three separate poisons allegedly found in Verna's brain and stomach, but the girl was nearly 6 months pregnant, a fact no one in her family was aware of.

No container was found near her body that might have held the poison, and because Verna was dry and clean, and her corpse posed in such a serene position, police were convinced that she had died elsewhere and someone had placed her body where it was found. This was pretty much confirmed when doctors admitted that once Verna ingested the poison, she would have been incapable of walking. It appeared that Verna Delp had been murdered, but who would have wanted the pretty girl dead?

Police immediately questioned Carl Bloom, Verna's pow-wow doctor, but he denied having seen the girl on Friday. This, however, contradicted what Verna's father had to say. When his daughter failed to return home, he had gone to Bloom's house himself, looking for her. Bloom had told the man that Verna had left immediately after her visit, but then added that he had heard a girl was found dead in a field—hours before Verna's body was found—and from the description, he thought it might be her.

Investigating Bloom further, police learned that Verna had been to see him at least nine times in just the past few weeks. Questioned further, Bloom finally admitted to authorities, that yes, he had treated Verna on the day she disappeared, but he denied giving her the "magic writings" found pinned to her breast. Bloom then went into seclusion, hired an attorney, and refused to cooperate any further with the police.

The authorities quickly became frustrated with the case. Not only wasn't Bloom talking, but neither was anyone else for fear the pow-wow man would cast a spell on them if they did. But despite those problems, police were still building a case against the witch doctor. An anonymous letter came to headquarters explaining the bizarre notes found with the body. According to the letter, N. I. R. constituted a charm against robbers and murderers in the "hex ritual," giving further credence to the notion that Verna's death was related to black magic. Police had also come across a witness who saw Bloom leave his house on the day Verna disappeared with an unidentified female, and then return after an hour or so alone. Another witness saw Bloom driving in the vicinity of the gun club that same day, again with an unidentified female. Even more damning were the following facts: Verna was found on a Saturday and Bloom was seen on the gun club grounds near the shed on that same Saturday morning *before* her body was discovered, Bloom had been one of the first on the scene after the body was found, Bloom had returned to the club that afternoon to participate in a shoot in plain sight of the authorities investigating the death.

It was the theory of the police that Verna had enlisted the aid of Bloom to cast a spell that would end her pregnancy. Bloom had probably taken Verna to the isolated shed where he gave her "mystical potions" that he claimed would induce an abortion. When Bloom botched the job, however, and Verna died, the pow-wow doctor had panicked. It was believed he left Verna's corpse in the shed overnight, which would account for why the body wasn't wet after the torrential downpour on Friday evening, and then returned early Saturday morning to move it outside.

Police finally arrested Bloom, and although they had a strong circumstantial case against him, a judge decided it was not enough to convict the man and he was released. Bloom returned to his home and continued practicing "medicine" for all his loyal patients.

And then of course, there was the most notorious and sensational pow-wow murder in all of the United States: the murder of Nelson D. Rehmeyer.

In the winter of 1928, Nelson Rehmeyer was a sixty-year-old farmer living alone on a small isolated farm located about four miles from the town of Shrewsbury. Although Rehmeyer and his wife had separated seven years earlier, they were still on friendly terms, and lived only about a mile apart. On the evening of November 26, 1928, two men appeared at Mrs. Rehmeyer's house inquiring as to the whereabouts of her husband, but neglecting to tell her what they wanted him for. Three days later, Nelson Rehmeyer was found lying dead on his kitchen floor, his body burned and charred beyond recognition.

Luckily, Rehmeyer's wife had recognized one of the two individuals who had come looking for her husband as twenty-eight-year-old John Blymire, a local pow-wow doctor who dabbled in the art of black magic. Police quickly arrested Blymire for the murder, along with two of his companions, seventeen-year-old Wilbert Hess and fourteen-year-old John Curry. The story these three individuals went on to tell would become one of the most bizarre ever heard in the history of American Crime.

It all began, so the three claimed, when Wilbert Hess's father, Milton, hired John Blymire to cast a spell on a neighbor who denied him access to a certain piece of property. John Blymire, whose father, grandfather, and great-grandfather were also pow-wows, readily agreed, and charged Milton Hess $50.00 to do the deed. Nothing, however was done, and when Hess complained, Blymire told him that the reason his own spell wasn't working was because the neighbor had hired Nelson Rehmeyer to cast a "counter-spell" against him.

Now, it seemed, not only was Milton Hess under the hex, but so was John Blymire, and Blymire quickly began feeling the effects of it. He became ill, weak, and was unable to sleep. Soon, other pow-wows confirmed his suspicion that it was Nelson Rehmeyer who had him cursed. The pow-wows told Blymire the only way to break Rehmeyer's hex was to obtain a copy of the old man's book entitled *The Long Lost Friend*[7]—considered a type of black magic bible used by witches—or procure a lock of the man's hair and bury it eight feet deep behind his barn.

Recruiting his fourteen-year-old co-worker, John Curry, to help, the two men went first to Rehmeyer's wife's house, and not finding him there, traveled over to Nelson's house itself. According to Blymire, they asked Nelson Rehmeyer to give them his copy of *The Long Lost Friend,* but the old man refused.

Although many people insisted that Nelson Rehmeyer dabbled in the art of black magic and pow-wow, there is no real evidence to support this. It's just as likely that he was simply an elderly man living out his life on his isolated farm. Whatever the truth, Nelson Rehmeyer insisted to Curry and Blymire that he didn't own a copy of *The Long Lost Friend*, but neither of them believed him.

The next day, Tuesday, November 27, 1928, John Blymire and John Curry went shopping to buy a length of rope, and then traveled up to the Hess farm. There, they told the family that they would need help in securing either the book, or a lock of Nelson Rehmeyer's hair, and young Wilbert, feeling he had to go for "the good of us all," agreed to accompany them.

---

[7] By John George Hohman, first published in 1820.

When the trio arrived at Rehmeyer's farm, they found the house in complete darkness. Nelson Rehmeyer was sound asleep when he was startled awake by furious pounding on his kitchen door. After allowing the three youths in, an argument broke out when Rehmeyer again insisted he didn't have a copy of *The Long Lost Friend*.

After turning his back on the group, John Blymire suddenly lunged at Nelson Rehmeyer and tackled him to the ground. After a brief struggle, both men managed to get back to their feet, and it was then that John Blymire picked up a wooden kitchen chair and broke it over Rehmeyer's head.

Fourteen-year-old John Curry, terrified as he watched the scene unfold before his eyes, later told police that the "witch" seemed to gain strength the more he was beaten. Grabbing a log used for the cooking stove, Curry jumped in and began bludgeoning the old man about the head. When Rehmeyer finally collapsed, Curry kicked him in the stomach as well.

With Rehmeyer incapacitated on the kitchen floor, John Blymire called for the rope. Hess and Curry handed it to him, expecting him to tie the old man up, but were surprised to see Blymire wrap the cord around Rehmeyer's neck and pull it tight. When Rehmeyer was no longer moving, the three youths trussed his hands and feet and then ransacked the house, allegedly looking for his copy of *The Long Lost Friend*, which they failed to find.

Without the book, the three youths knew they would have to get a lock of Nelson Rehmeyer's hair, but his head was battered and bloody, and none of the boys wanted to touch it. Blymire, however, told them the lock of hair was no longer necessary; the witch was dead, he said gleefully, and the spell now broken.

Wilbert Hess took the feather tick off of Nelson Rehmeyer's bed, and threw it atop the dead man's corpse. John Curry grabbed an oil lamp, took off the burner, poured oil on the body, struck a match and dropped it on the bundle. The boys assumed the fire would burn down the house, eliminating any evidence of their crime, but they were wrong. The fire burned Nelson Rehmeyer to a crisp, and left a hole in the middle of his kitchen floor, but it did not burn down his house.

The three youths were quickly tried for the gruesome murder and just as swiftly convicted. John Blymire and John Curry each received life sentences, and Wilbert Hess received a prison term of ten to twenty years.

And now there was Susan Mummey's death; another murder involving a suspected witch and a hex. Authorities simply shook their heads, wondering if the craziness would ever end.

~*~*~

On the morning of March 22, 1934, Susan Mummey was laid to rest in the cemetery at Ringtown, and later that same afternoon Albert Shinsky eagerly re-enacted her murder for the police. Throughout the reenactment Shinsky showed no remorse; instead, he seemed happy, well-pleased with himself, and almost giddy.

After showing the investigators where he had parked his jitney on that fateful night, Albert then led them on a two-mile trek through heavy woods. There was no pathway to speak of; the youth simply zigzagged throughout the forest, clambering over fallen trees, breaking through brush and scrub, and forcing his way through the thick undergrowth that had yet to show any signs of spring. Finally, after more than an hour, the group broke through the woods into a clearing.

There before them sat the Mummey farmhouse, old, decaying, and spooky even in the brightness of day. The officers noticed that Albert Shinksy's body seemed to vibrate when he saw it. He stopped abruptly, gazing at the house, visibly trembling. Soon detective Buono nudged him, and Albert began to walk again, slowly, hesitantly, making his way ever nearer to the witch's abode.

"I had come to the conclusion that I'd have to kill her to break the spell." Albert said quietly, "So I crept up on the porch," he crouched down to show them how he had inched his way up the wooden steps, "and went to the window."

He stood slowly, pretending to peer into the window that was now covered with plywood. "I could see Susie by the lamplight, and Tavia [sic] standing next to her. She [Susan] was bending over, looking at the man who was sitting in the chair, and as I stood here, I heard a voice come down from the sky that said, 'shoot that woman.'" Albert hesitated for a moment before going on. "So I did," he said quietly. "I raised the gun and fired."

Albert turned toward the officers now, the look upon his face a combination of delight, ecstasy, and enlightenment. It was both deeply unnerving and bizarrely grotesque to the lawmen who stood with him.

"As soon as I saw her tumble over on her side," the young killer continued, "I felt something soothing pass over me. I knew right then that the spell had been broken."

Albert stood there for a moment, still lost in his pleasurable semi-trance, before gradually coming out of it. When he did, he looked around in confusion, as if surprised to find himself at the Mummey house. "I shot a second time," he said, "just to scare Tavia [sic] and the man, and then I left."

"What kind of weapon did you use?" he was asked.

"A 12-gauge shotgun," Albert answered, adding quickly, "but not mine. I borrowed it from a friend."

Detective Buono asked where the gun was now and Albert said, "I'll show you."

Once again, the young killer led the officers through the deep forest, to a spot where he had buried parts of the 12-gauge shotgun. He had obviously dismantled the weapon before hiding it under a pile of dead leaves.

After carefully slipping the gun pieces into a brown evidence bag, the officers returned their prisoner to the Schuylkill County jail and then drove over to Shinsky's friend's house to question him about the weapon. The friend confirmed Shinsky's story, but denied he had known what Albert wanted the gun for. There was no evidence that the friend was lying, and police believed him. From there, they drove over to pay a visit to Selena Bernstel, Albert Shinsky's nineteen-year-old fiancé.

Selena was a very pretty girl with dark hair and large brown eyes. She seemed devoted to her boyfriend, and was devastated over what had happened. When she spoke to the investigators, she did so through bitter tears.

"I knew something had happened," Selena sobbed, "because Albert seemed different and more gay since last Saturday. He acted as if something had been taken off of him."

"Selena," Detective Buono asked, "do you believe in the hex?"

The young girl dropped her eyes and shook her head slightly. "Not really," she began, sounding sincere, but then quickly added, "but I have no doubt that Albert was bewitched. Why, he wouldn't even kiss me when the spell was on him." She sounded as if that were proof positive that her fiancé had been cursed.

Asked how she had met Albert, Selena said that the two had met at a dance in Ringtown a few years earlier.

"He was sitting all alone in a corner, ignoring everyone, with his head drooping down, and a sad look about him," Selena said, but she had noticed him immediately, and pressured a friend to introduce them. The friend had, and although Selena had tried to talk to Albert, he had hardly responded to her. Still, Selena continued, "I took a liking to him right off, and even though he would barely speak to me, something wouldn't let me stop. I could feel myself getting all tingly."

She told the detectives that after talking for a while, she had insisted that Albert tell her what was wrong, and he finally had. According to him, Selena said, "There was some terrible old woman who had put a hex on him. He couldn't do anything right, or act like other people do. He told me about the green-eyed cat with a face like the witch that visited him. And he said when that happened, he would get awful hot and then freezing cold."

"And did you believe this?" one of the officers asked.

Despite the fact that Selena had claimed, only moments earlier, that she really didn't believe in the hex, she now looked up at her interrogators indignantly. "Sure I did. I believed him right off. Why shouldn't I? I had a cousin who was hexed once." She paused for a moment, and when she continued her voice took on a desperate tone. "You could tell something was horribly wrong with Albert and my cousin acted just the same way. My cousin used to be visited by the ghost of an old woman who cast a spell over her."

Selena appeared modestly embarrassed as she told the officers that she had found Albert to be very good looking and kind but that she had been forced to be the aggressor in the relationship. This was okay, however, because, "that way I thought the spirit of Mrs. Mummey would have no cause to visit Albert because he was entirely passive."

"What do you mean when you say you had to be the aggressor in the relationship?"

Selena sighed wearily. "I was always the one to ask Albert to go places. All the courting was up to me. If I had an extra quarter I'd ride over to see him on the bus. Most of his money went to pow-wow doctors to try and help him. Now and then he'd say what a dope I was to go out with him when other boys liked me too."

When they asked if she ever considered leaving him, Selena admitted, "Of course there were times when I got impatient, and even told him I was going to get another fellow, but at such times, Albert cried awful, and pleaded with me not to desert him. He said I was the only friend he had."

Selena shook her head and dabbed at her teary eyes with a lace hanky. "I couldn't have left him anyway," she cried, admitting, "Something about him had too strong a hold on me."

Shinsky's girlfriend described him as being like a "little puppy dog," or a "lost soul," and told her interrogators that, "When we went to the movies, often he'd fall asleep with his head on my shoulder. I'd stroke his head and cry and cry and not even see the picture."

Selena leaned back in her chair and eyed the men sitting across from her. Then, almost secretively, she leaned forward again and whispered, "Things began happening to me at night too."

Raising his eyebrows, detective Buono asked, "What do you mean? What things?"

Well, Selena continued, "about twice a month I'd wake up to see Albert, plain as day, standing at the foot of my bed. He'd hold his side, his face twisted in pain, and he'd hold out his other arm to me. But when I stirred, his figure would leave. Each time this happened, I'd find out that he had one of those terrible visits from the cat or the old woman. He told me she would be dressed in black with a white light outlining her body, leering and leering at him."

"Selena," one of the officer's suddenly blurted, his voice betraying his disbelief, "did you truly believe all this?"

The young girl nodded her head vigorously. It was all true, she exclaimed. "Once he told me that the witch made him go to her cabin every now and then, and that he would feel paralyzed and could only move towards her place. He said he begged and begged her to lift the spell but she wouldn't."

Selena looked like a girl in complete misery as she related these bizarre tales, and then she broke down and began sobbing uncontrollably. "I asked him several times to marry me," she cried, "but he always said the witch wouldn't let him."

One of the officers reached for a new hanky, and after giving it to the distraught girl, who took a few moments to compose herself, he gently asked her about her fiancé's demeanor after the crime. Immediately, Selena perked up and stopped crying.

"The night after the murder," she said, smiling for the first time, "Albert took me to the movies. I was tired, and for a change it was me who fell asleep on his shoulder. When I woke up, he was kissing me!" She paused for a moment, appearing deliriously happy. "Boy was I surprised. It had always been the other way with us. Then the next day, Monday, we went to the movies again, and when we got home from the show, Albert insisted on us staying up in the yard until 3:00 in the morning. He was cuddling me and laughing all the time. He kept talking about how happy we were and how swell the moon was. I knew something must have happened because he was so changed, but he wouldn't tell me what, and I was too dizzy with gladness to care!"

~*~*~

Although the press was having a hard time finding anyone in the area who would admit to a belief in witchcraft and the hex, things were happening behind the scenes that made it perfectly clear that a large number of people still believed in it.

A small group of men and women started a defense fund for Albert Shinsky, which grew at an alarming rate. Donations poured in from all over Schuylkill County and beyond, and detective Louis Buono, albeit reluctantly, admitted that since the murder, no less than three other men had approached him to say that Susan Mummey had also cast a spell on them. The men insisted that the spell was broken the moment Albert Shinsky killed her.

Meanwhile, the killer of the purported witch remained in the Schuylkill County jail, appearing happy and content, and willing to give interviews to anyone who inquired. When asked if he were worried about the charges pending against him, Shinsky shook his head and smiled.

"I'm at peace now," he said pleasantly, "because I've finally broken that woman's spell over me."

When District Attorney Leroy Enterline charged the youth with first degree murder and demanded the death penalty, Albert Shinsky simply shrugged. "I know I'm going to be electrocuted now," he said, "but I don't care. I have peace."

Confronted with the fact that some people thought him irrational—even crazy—the young killer of Susan Mummey simply sneered. "I'm fine," he protested. "I'm just greatly relieved that the spell has been broken."

Selena, too, was fond of talking to the press, and usually did so after visiting her fiancé in jail. On March 24, she came outside the prison and turned to face the cameras. "Albert is fine," she told the eager reporters, "and he just told me today that it was wonderful not to have the spirits bothering him anymore."

"Selena," one of the reporters called out, "is it true that you donated your week's pay to Albert's defense fund?"

Selena smiled. "I make $9.00 a week working in a shirt factory," she said, nodding her head, "and it's all I have, but it's his if it will help him. I love him, and I intend to stand by him." Turning to leave, she paused for a moment and then turned back. "You know, I begged him to let me marry him now so I could stand with him and help him, but he refused me." She appeared heartbroken as she said it.

~*~*~

On March 26, 1934, Doctor Walter G. Bowers, a psychiatrist and superintendent of the Schuylkill County Hospital for the Insane, drove to the Pottsville jail to interview Albert Shinsky. The two men talked for two hours, the prisoner holding nothing back about Susan Mummey, the curse she had put on him, and her murder. Not surprisingly, before the doctor finally left he had already formed the opinion that Albert Shinsky was dreadfully insane.

Bowers believed the young killer was suffering from a form of mental illness called Dementia Praecox, a condition characterized by vivid hallucinations. It was his belief that Shinsky should not be tried, but rather judged insane and sent to Farview State Hospital for the criminally insane located in the northeastern part of state, in a small town called Waymart.

Phoning District Attorney Leroy Enterline, Bowers told him of his assessment and urged him to recommend to the court that a sanity commission be appointed. Enterline, who also believed that Shinsky was insane, readily agreed, but both men knew it wouldn't be that easy.

Curiously, at that time, any application for a sanity commission in Schuylkill County routinely came from prison wardens, not doctors or attorneys, and William Watson, the warden of the Pottsville jail, was having none of it. He had already told Leroy Enterline that he didn't think Shinsky was crazy, and what's more, he was sick and tired of the enjoyment his prisoner was receiving from the publicity his crime had generated.

Enterline was dismayed by Watson's attitude, and perhaps hoping not to entice the warden's anger, he appeared secretive when he spoke to the press.

"I have just received Doctor Bowers' written report on the mental condition of Albert Shinsky," Enterline said, "but I do not care to divulge its contents immediately. After giving the report due consideration, I shall be ready to act on it."

Doctor Bowers, however, had no fear of upsetting the warden at the Pottsville jail, and no qualms with telling the media exactly what he thought. "My report declares Shinsky insane," he said bluntly, "and recommends an appointment by the court of a sanity commission to examine the lad."

When Albert was told what Doctor Bowers had said about him, he seemed amused. "Oh him," he laughed, "he asked a lot of funny questions."

"But what if you're found insane?" one of the reporters wanted to know.

Shinsky laughed again. "That's a good one!" he cried. "I'm okay. Everything is swell now. I feel swell."

"But suppose they send you to the big house?"

Shinsky seemed to consider this for a moment, and then shrugged his shoulders. "I don't care. Everything is swell now. Anyone can see that I'm alright now that I'm not hexed anymore. I feel great now that she's dead."

Warden Watson, angered and disgusted by Shinsky's impromptu press conferences, immediately barred his prisoner from having any visitors or conducting interviews. Then, Watson faced the press himself. Openly scoffing at Doctor Bowers' assessment of his prisoner, Watson said angrily, "Shinsky's been acting normal while here in my jail, and I have seen nothing to indicate he is insane."

On March 28, however, Watson himself did a complete turnabout and petitioned the court for a sanity hearing on Albert Shinsky. Judge Henry Houck then appointed Doctor Bowers and Doctor J.B. Rodgers, former Schuylkill County Medical Director, to examine the prisoner again.

Two days later, on March 30, the two doctors did so, and reported their findings to the judge on April 9, 1934. They each agreed that Albert Shinsky was suffering from Dementia Praecox, manifested by paranoid delusions, and declared him incompetent to stand trial.

Most people agreed with the doctors' assessment, but not Albert Shinsky, who was greatly upset by it. The young prisoner was desperately eager to go to trial so he could be acquitted of the crime, and "marry my girl."

That, however, was not to be. On April 13, 1934—Friday the thirteenth—Judge Houck ordered Albert Shinsky remanded to Farview State Hospital for the criminally insane. If anyone was under the impression that the judge's decision meant that Albert Shinksky was getting away with murder—and would do a few years in a cushy hospital—they were greatly mistaken.

Farview had its own reputation among convicts, and a slew of nicknames to go with it, the most often used being "the place of no return." It was rumored that people went to the institution for what was deemed a "brief stay," and were never seen again, and in some instances those rumors were true. In fact, by the mid-1970s Farview would become the subject of an explosive scandal that would nearly rock the institution from its very foundation. So serious would the allegations be that not only would they threaten to close the hospital down for good, but also to send many of its top officials directly to prison.

It was the Philadelphia Inquirer which first broke the story after two of its investigative journalists, Acel Moore and Wendell Rawls Jr, began looking into allegations of patient mistreatment at the hospital. What Moore and Rawls uncovered would win each of them a Pulitzer Prize for investigative journalism, and result in a bestselling book on the subject, entitled *Cold Storage*.[8]

Their investigation uncovered a prison posing as a hospital, where brutality and abuse were the norm, guards ran the show, and medical treatment was virtually non-existent. Farview, so it seemed, was little more than a warehouse where violence and death reigned. There were stories of human cockfights between patients—fought to the death—set up simply to amuse the staff, and tales of guards repeatedly and horrifically beating patients, many of whom died as a result. There were also allegations of men being murdered and their deaths attributed to natural causes, and rumors of secret and hidden graves on the hospital grounds. Gambling, homosexuality, and thefts of inmates' belongings ran rampant, and it was discovered that patients who had been sent to the hospital for a 30 or 60 day evaluation, were still there *decades* later.

The list of inhumane conditions existing at Farview went on and on, and eventually led to a Grand Jury investigation that deemed most of the allegations uncovered by Moore and Rawls to be true. Once the story broke, things changed drastically at Farview, but that was more than forty years after Susan Mummey was murdered. Albert Shinsky, of course, would be going there long before anything changed.

---

[8] Published by Simon and Shuster February 26, 1980

On April 24, 1934, Albert's family went to the jail to say goodbye and the next day Sheriff Thomas Evans and his deputy drove their prisoner to Farview. Shinsky seemed his relaxed and carefree self as he climbed into the waiting vehicle, although he was disappointed that Selena was not there to see him off. District Attorney Enterline was there, however, eager to tell reporters that if Shinsky ever regained his sanity he'd be waiting to try him for murder. The doctors who had examined the hexed youth, however, deemed the chances of that ever happening as "extremely remote."

It seemed, at that point, that the Shinksy case was finally over. Albert had disappeared into the bowels of the mental asylum, where it was reported he was a model patient who caused little trouble, and the small town of Ringtown gradually forgot about him. It would be 34 years before anything new was heard about the killer of Susan Mummey. In 1968, a Shenandoah attorney, William J. Krencewicz, became aware of the case and decided to try to help Albert. Enlisting the aid of the Shenandoah Evening Herald newspaper, the compassionate attorney made an effort to have the inmate re-examined by psychiatrists in the hopes of having him declared sane.

Less than a year later, a book came out on the Nelson Rehmeyer case, entitled *Hex*,[9] by Arthur H. Lewis, which mentioned very briefly, the murder of Susan Mummey. Lewis interviewed Albert Shinsky for his book, and Shinsky, who was then fifty-seven-years-old, said he understood if the psychiatrists declared him sane he'd have to stand trial for killing Mrs. Mummey. It was a risk, the mental patient said, that he was willing to take. The murder was something he claimed to deeply regret, and something for which he had been sorry ever since he committed it. "I was a stupid, foolish, superstitious young man when I did it," he said, adding, "but I do think I've been punished enough."

---

[9] Published by Simon and Shuster / Trident Press February 1969

Apparently, however, others did not feel the same way. It wasn't until October of 1975, *forty-one* years after he entered Farview State Hospital that Albert Shinsky finally left it. Brought back to Schuylkill County for a hearing to determine his competency to stand trial, Shinsky was housed in the Wernersville State Hospital to await the court's decision. From there, he told reporters, "I intend to make an adequate defense to clear the whole thing up."

In January, 1976, Schuylkill County Judge James J. Curran ruled that Shinsky was competent to stand trial, clearing the way for him to be tried for the murder of Susan Mummey. But if Shinsky was tried for Susan's murder, the newspapers of the time didn't report on it. Shinsky's name never appeared in the press again. He had spent at least forty-two years in prison for killing Susan Mummey, and it's possible that after being adjudged sane, he was released for time served.

What is known about Albert Shinsky is that he was a free man, living back in Ringtown, at the time of his death on May 1, 1983. He was seventy-five-years-old by then, and described as a kind man who kept mainly to himself. Having spent the majority of his life in a mental institution, Albert Shinsky never married. He was buried in a local cemetery, next to his parents in the family plot, his life and his crime, all but forgotten.

Postscript:
I chose to write about the Shinsky case because, unlike the Nelson Rehmeyer case, which has been told in great detail, there has been little written about the murder of Susan Mummey.

I was unable to find out what happened to Tovillia Mummey, who seems to have simply vanished from history, nor was I able to discover what became of Albert's fiancé, Selena Bernstel.

The fate of the three killers of Nelson Rehmeyer, however, is well-known:
    Wilbert Hess was paroled on June 16, 1939, and John Curry less than two weeks later, on June 29, 1939.

Wilbert Hess returned home to live with his parents, and became a well-respected citizen of the town.

John Curry, who was only fourteen-years-old when he participated in the murder of Nelson Rehmeyer, and only twenty-four when he made parole, went on to marry and have a family. Curry also fought during WWII, winning a bronze star for his efforts.

John Blymire, who served a much longer sentence than his two companions, was not released from prison until February 10, 1953. Afterwards, he took a job as an apartment manager, lived frugally, and eventually saved enough money to buy his own house.

The house where Nelson Rehmeyer met his death still stands today, and last I heard, there were plans to turn it into a tourist attraction.

Are there those who still believe in the hex and practice pow-wow? That's a question I don't have an answer for. I do know, however, that up until at least the late 1960s there were still pow-wow doctors who advertised their trade. I doubt many would publicly admit to a belief in the hex today, or to being endowed with the power to break such spells, but then, traditions and beliefs often die hard.

THE GHOST OF FAIRMOUNT PARK

(Philadelphia PA. The brutal murder of Rose McCloskey.)

The three youths nudged each other, snickering as they watched the man weave down the middle of the street, stumble, regain his footing, and then lurch forward again. They couldn't make out his features—the dim gloom of the night made it difficult for them to see—but it seemed clear from his stagger that the man was drunk. As he continued to zigzag along the road, the boys saw him suddenly stop and grasp his head with both hands, as if in great despair. He seemed agitated as he stood there wobbling slightly, then slowly dropped his hands and pitched forward once again.

The man took a few more steps before noticing the three boys and immediately turned towards them. He moved quickly, still weaving, his arms reaching out in supplication, and the teens, who were initially amused by this little show, suddenly began to feel afraid. They each took a step back, their laughter abruptly ceasing, their cocky attitude instantly gone. What was the man doing, they wondered? What did he want?

The gap was quickly closing between them. Each step brought the man closer, bringing him into focus and convincing the boys that they had been mistaken about his condition. He wasn't drunk; he was dazed, confused, and gravely injured.

Blood saturated the man's face and head, and matted his hair into thick, glistening ropes. Although he stared directly at the three boys, his eyes were glazed and unfocused, and obviously not registering anything he saw. The man was out of it, delirious, as he collapsed into their outstretched arms, and they gently lowered him to the frozen pavement.

"Jesus," one of them exclaimed, "Are you okay buddy? What happened?"

The boys didn't know if the man could hear them or not, but he didn't appear to understand anything they said. Still, he opened his mouth as if to answer, but his words came out disjointed and jumbled, and intermingled with a stream of bright red blood. Blood was also gushing from several gaping wounds to his scalp, and as one of the boys peered closer at his injuries, he quickly recoiled in horror. It looked like the man's brain was oozing from his skull.

"We have to get him help," the boy blurted, fear evident in his voice. "He's going to die right here."

There was a hospital only a few blocks away and panicked, the three youths hoisted the man to his feet, and half carried, half dragged him there.

The emergency personnel took one look at the blood-soaked man being ushered into their emergency room and immediately called for a stretcher. Strapping the man to the gurney, they rushed him through a pair of swinging doors, leaving instructions with the nurse to call the police and make sure the three teens didn't leave.

The police arrived within minutes and questioned the three closely, but the youths claimed they didn't know who the man was or what had happened to him; they had simply found him wandering dazed in the street. No one else had been around when they discovered him, and they had no idea where he had come from or where he had been.

Leading the police back to the street where they had encountered the injured man, the three boys watched excitedly as the officers followed the blood trail that zigzagged up the pavement. The trail ended near a four foot high hedge bordering Fairmount Park—a popular destination for young lovers—and authorities noted that this section of the hedge was clearly disturbed. The shrubs looked mangled; their limbs bent and broken, their greenery dotted with what appeared to be freshly shed blood.

It seemed apparent that the injured man had crashed through them, either while trying to get away from his assailant or as he wandered helplessly in his confused state, but the darkness of the night made any effort to follow the trail nearly impossible. Authorities realized they would have to wait until dawn to begin a thorough search, and quickly decided to head back over to the hospital to see if their victim could provide any details of his attack.

Once there, however, Police Captain Harry Heanley, and Murder Squad Detective Joseph Summerdale were sorely disappointed to find that their victim wasn't expected to live. Doctors told the officer that the man had sustained at least three violent blows to the head that had resulted in a compound fracture of the skull, and since being admitted had lapsed into a coma.

A search of their victim's clothing revealed identification in the name of Dennis Boyle, age thirty, and four crisp, new $1.00 bills. The undisturbed money and the fact that the man was wearing a moderately expensive gold watch led the officers to rule out robbery as a motive. Apparently, Dennis Boyle hadn't been mugged, but someone obviously had a reason to want the man dead.

The address provided on Boyle's identification led police to a West Philadelphia apartment where they arrived around 1:00 am. Expecting anyone inside to be sound asleep, they were surprised when their loud knocks were immediately answered by a worried young woman. The girl looked distressed and identified herself as Mary Callahan, a sister to Dennis Boyle.

Mary told the officers that Dennis had left the apartment earlier that evening, around 9:00 pm, saying he was taking his nineteen-year-old fiancé, Rose McCloskey, to the movies. Mary knew that Rose had a curfew, and she had expected Dennis to be home no later than 11:30. When he didn't arrive, she had waited up for him, becoming more worried and anxious by the moment. She had been pacing the floor, trying to quell the rising panic that was threatening to consume her, when the police had knocked at her door.

Dennis Boyle had been discovered wandering in the street at approximately 10:00 pm—only an hour after he had left his apartment—and police wondered if he would have had time to meet up with his girlfriend before the attack. They asked Dennis' sister to tell them about his girlfriend, and Mary described Rose as a sweet girl who worked as a cashier in a downtown department store. Despite the fact that eleven years separated Rose and Dennis, Mary continued, the two got along wonderfully and had been dating for the past two years. Dennis had come to Philadelphia from New York, where he had worked as a doorman in a theatre, but he had been unable to find a job since he arrived. Rose's mother, Annie McCloskey, who owned a delicatessen in the city, did not approve of her daughter's relationship with Dennis, but that didn't matter to her brother or to Rose; the two were in love, and planned to marry as soon as he found work.

Mary insisted she had no idea who might have attacked her brother, saying that as far as she knew, Dennis had no enemies. He also would have been an unlikely target for robbery, since he rarely had any money these days. But besides that, she added, Dennis wasn't stupid; had someone tried to mug him, he would have handed over anything he had.

The police took notes as they talked with the distraught woman, and then offered to escort her over to Presbyterian Hospital where her brother had been admitted. Mary Callahan nodded gratefully and reached for her coat.

Turning back to the officers, she suddenly asked, "Where is Rose? What did she say happened?"

The two detectives glanced at each other and shrugged. They had no idea where Rose McCloskey was. They hadn't even known she existed until Mary Callahan told them about her.

After detouring to drop Dennis Boyle's sister at the hospital, the officers drove directly to the McCloskey home and pounded on their door. Although it was after 2:00 am, their repeated knocks went unanswered, a fact the investigators found both odd and troubling. It was a Wednesday night—technically early Thursday morning—January 5, 1933, and bitterly cold outside. Where could an entire family be on such a bone-chilling night, and at such a dreadful hour?

They wondered if Rose McCloskey was missing too, and if her family was out looking for her. Or—another possibility—could Rose's family somehow be involved in the attack? Could a confrontation between Rose's parents and Dennis Boyle—perhaps over the couple's relationship—have erupted into violence and the McCloskey's since fled?

The officers soon had their answer when they called headquarters to report that the McCloskey family couldn't be found. They discovered that Rose's parents, Annie and Patrick, were right there at the station, filing a missing person's report on their teenage daughter. They stated that Rose had left her mother's delicatessen earlier that evening, around 9:00 pm, saying she was "going to meet a friend." Annie McCloskey had known the "friend" was Dennis Boyle, even though her daughter hadn't mention him by name.

Annie went on to explain that she knew Rose was dating Dennis, but her daughter rarely spoke about him because she knew how her mother felt about the relationship. It was no secret in the McCloskey household, however, that the couple had been seeing each other and planned to marry in the near future.

The officers asked Mrs. McCloskey why she had a problem with the two of them dating, and Annie quickly explained that it had nothing to do with Dennis Boyle himself. In fact, she said, she found Dennis to be a very nice young man. What bothered Annie McCloskey was the vast age difference between the couple. Dennis Boyle was thirty-years-old, and her daughter was just a teenager. Annie simply couldn't fathom what the two of them could have in common.

Continuing with her story, Annie said that after Rose had left her shop earlier that evening, she had not seen or heard from her daughter again. When Rose failed to return home, Annie was afraid that the two might have eloped, and upset by the thought, she and her husband contacted the police. It was then that they learned about Dennis Boyle being in Presbyterian Hospital and not expected to live, and their fear had quickly turned to dread. Where was their daughter, they asked desperately?

The parents of the missing girl sat stunned and in shock, clinging to each other as they sobbed in fear. Presently, Annie turned to her husband and buried her head against his chest. She was repeating something over and over again, but her voice was muffled against Patrick's shirt, and it took a moment for him to understand what she was saying.

"I wish they had eloped," Annie sobbed. "I wish they had eloped. *Oh God, how I wish they had eloped.*"

~*~*~

Although no one was certain where the young couple had planned to go that evening, Dennis Boyle had been found wandering in the street not far from Fairmount Park, a vast tract of land consisting of 9200 acres of untamed wilderness, lush vegetation, and dense forest.

Fairmount Park had originally been part of a country estate owned by Robert Morris, one of Philadelphia's most-famous sons, and a man who played a large role in our countries independence. Morris had not only helped finance the Revolutionary War, but he was also one, (of only two people), to sign the three most important documents in American history; the Declaration of Independence, the Articles of the Confederation, and the United States Constitution. In later years, after a number of bad investments, Morris went bankrupt and sold his land to Henry Pratt, a merchant trader who built a mansion on the property. Pratt called his new home Lemon Hill Estates, and eventually, in 1843, it, and several other properties, were purchased by the city council, and Fairmount Park was born.

The park was a tranquil place; consisting of beautiful gardens, picnic areas, and countless walking trails that meandered off into thick woods. The vast trees of the forest often formed tunnels so dark that even in the bright of day one was left feeling twilight had descended upon him. Bordering this green oasis on one side was the Schuylkill River, its rushing waters dotted by small islets popular with those who enjoyed swimming, boating or water sports.

Fairmount Park was a peaceful retreat from the noise and congestion of the bustling city which lay just outside its boundaries, and a place that encompassed everything a nature enthusiast could want. It provided relief from the sweltering heat of summer, sledding and skating in the winter months, and privacy all year long to anyone who wanted it.

When Dennis Boyle was found wandering just outside the park's perimeter on January 4, 1933, police suspected that he and Rose may have been there earlier, and it was a thought that concerned them. They knew that even when the river was layered with ice, and the trees stood stark and bare, the park was still a popular destination for those willing to brave the cold. They knew something else as well; for the past two years, someone had been stalking the women and lovers of Fairmount Park.

~*~*~

Like Central Park in New York and Highland Park in Los Angeles, Fairmount Park in Philadelphia has always had its fair share of crime. Today, few young couples would venture to take a stroll through *any* metropolitan park after dark, but in 1933, that was not the case. Of course, crime still occurred in Fairmount Park at that time, but it was rarely violent, and the park was still considered a safe place to visit, even at night.

At the time Rose McCloskey went missing, and Dennis Boyle was found wandering in the street, authorities knew—although the general public did not—that the crime rate in Fairmount Park had been escalating. Young, single women—and sometimes even couples—were being stalked and often accosted by a group of young men police referred to as "a gang of thugs."

Initially, these incidents amounted to little more than mischievous behavior and scare-tactics; people would be stared at, followed, mocked and harassed. Gradually, however, the crimes advanced to include petty theft—pickpockets and purse snatchings—and then outright intimidation. On at least one occasion, the group had surrounded a terrified woman, snatched her purse, and played catch with it over her head before running off to discard it a hundred yards away.

This type of action was still considered prankish by the police, but they knew that the pranks were becoming more and more brazen each day. There were reports of pushing and shoving, threats of future violence, and even several vicious attacks and sexual assaults. Numerous people had reported being mugged and beaten, and at least twice in recent months, single young women had been attacked from behind, pushed to the ground, and sexually molested, if not actually raped.

Even more alarming to the police was an incident that occurred nearly two years earlier, when on August 15, 1931 pretty twenty-one-year-old Helen Loftus and her twenty-four-year-old fiancé, Maurice Scott, decided to rent a canoe and take a trip down the Schuylkill River. It was a beautiful day, the river was calm, and both Helen and Maurice were expert swimmers, each having competed and won prizes for their swimming abilities while still in school.

Launching their canoe from Fairmount Park around 11:00 am, the young couple had planned to be on the water until late afternoon and then have dinner in Philadelphia before returning home. Maurice had just gotten paid the day before and had somewhere between $40.00 and $50.00 in his wallet to use for the excursion.

Helen and Maurice had each grown up in the small town of Carbondale, approximately 150 miles north of Philadelphia, where the majority of their families still lived. Carbondale was "coal country," and after graduating from high-school, Maurice took a job with the Hudson Coal Company at their Coalbrook Colliery in Carbondale. He and Helen had dated all through school and continued to do so, until Helen's mother took her daughter and moved to Philadelphia. After only a week or so, finding that he missed Helen terribly, Maurice had quit his job and decided to follow. He rented a small room in the city, took a job with the National Biscuit Company, and asked Helen to marry him, setting their wedding date for the coming November.

On that hot August afternoon, when the two decided to take a canoe trip down the Schuylkill River, both Helen and Maurice were looking forward to their life together, and their future. Each of them awoke in a good mood and eager to begin their day—unaware that it would be their last.

When the young couple failed to return home that evening, their families reported their disappearance to the police, and an intensive search was immediately begun. On August 16th their canoe was found, beached upside down on the bank of the river, but there was no sign of the missing pair. A second search was ordered, this one on the grounds of Fairmount Park, to coincide with that being done on the water.

Two days later, on the morning of August 18, 1931, the body of Maurice Scott was found washed up on an island in the Schuylkill River, still within the confines of the park. Scott appeared to have been badly beaten, his body covered with cuts and bruises, his head battered and gashed. It was discovered that a wristwatch he had received from the Hudson Coal Company was missing, and although his wallet was found neatly tucked away in his back pocket, it was devoid of any money.

There was no sign of Maurice's girlfriend, and it was another twelve hours before the body of Helen Loftus was found floating a little farther downstream, caught up on some branches near an overflow dam. The condition of Helen's corpse indicated a vicious beating far more brutal than even that of Maurice Scott. Helen's body was lacerated with open cuts, and bruises indicated her face had been repeatedly struck, her jaw broken, and her skull fractured. Although police didn't know if Helen had carried any money with her that day, her wristwatch, just like her fiancé's, was also missing.

After authorities had photographed the scene, both bodies were released to the coroner for autopsy. It was quickly established that Maurice Scott had died from drowning but Helen was discovered to have no water in her lungs, and her death was attributed to blunt force trauma of the head. Despite this finding, First Deputy Coroner Arthur Sellers ruled the deaths accidental—the result of a boating accident—and authorities accepted the ruling and quickly closed the case.

Helen's father, Martin Loftus, was incredulous and outraged, insisting that his daughter and her fiancé had been murdered, and demanding a full investigation. How, he thundered, could police call these deaths an accident? Martin Loftus had questions that no one seemed willing or able to answer.

How could a boating accident occur when the water was so calm and serene that day? How had Helen and Maurice received such violent and vicious injuries? Why didn't anyone witness the accident—it was a beautiful, sunny Saturday, and both the park and the river were crammed with people. How could Maurice have lost his money, but manage to get his wallet back inside his pants pocket? How could the canoe have floated to shore, climbed halfway up the riverbank, and then turned itself over? If it were a boating accident, then why was there no water in Helen's lungs?

Martin Loftus's questions were good ones—valid and to the point—but they fell on deaf ears. The coroner refused to change the manner of death, and the police declined to re-open the case. As Helen was being buried in Philadelphia, and Maurice's body was being brought back to Carbondale to be interred there, the story quickly became old news and dropped from the newspapers.

And there the case may have ended, had it not been for Martin Loftus, who was an influential man with contacts in high places. Helen's father immediately hired a Private Investigator to look into his daughter and her fiancé's death, and enlisted the aid of his brother to contact Pennsylvania Governor Gifford Pinchot, and Deputy Superintendent of the Pennsylvania State Police, S. M. Wilhelm.

Loftus wielded his power and soon had a coroner's inquest looking into the deaths of Helen and Maurice. Within days, a verdict was returned listing their deaths as a result of murder "at the hands of persons unknown."

Doctor Richard Burke, coroner's physician, testified at the hearing that Helen had died from repeated blows to the head by a hatchet—or similar type weapon—and that Maurice had sustained his injuries in the same way. A theory for the crime was also offered: since Maurice's body had been recovered floating near a small island, it was believed that the couple had probably stopped there during their trip where they encountered their killer(s). Maurice had most likely been assaulted first, viciously beaten—though not killed—and then thrown in the water unconscious where he subsequently drowned. Helen, it was believed, had probably been held on the island and sexually assaulted before being beaten to death and thrown in the water as well.

Police were unhappy that the deaths had been ruled murders, and in fact, after the Coroner's jury handed down their verdict, Captain Harry Heanley told the press; "I'm still convinced this was a boating accident. The police have washed their hands of the whole affair."

Despite these feelings, the authorities had no choice but to investigate the deaths, although they appeared to put little effort into their investigation. The case was already more than a year old and had since grown cold. Now, however, faced with a badly beaten man, and a missing teenage girl—two incidents that may have occurred in Fairmount Park, the same place where Helen Loftus and Maurice Scott had died—police began to wonder if they had made a grave mistake.

~*~*~

Authorities were searching Fairmount Park in a desperate attempt to find Rose McCloskey, but their efforts were being hampered by the bitter cold and the darkness of the night. It was early January in Eastern Pennsylvania, and the temperature hovered below the freezing mark. Flashlights and lanterns barely penetrated the gloom of the heavy woods, and shadows wreaked havoc with the searcher's minds.

Back at Presbyterian Hospital, officers sat vigil at the bedside of Dennis Boyle, hoping he might regain consciousness and tell them what had happened, but they were not optimistic. Doctors had already told them his chances for recovery were slim. Still, they waited and they hoped, knowing Dennis was the only one who could unlock the mystery to the case.

Some officers saw no need to wait for Dennis, however, and readily shared their own ideas of what they believed happened. Noting that Rose McCloskey was a beautiful girl—thin and attractive with raven colored hair and a smile that lit up her entire face—it seemed obvious to many that jealousy was most-likely the motive for the attack.

"Look," one of the detectives said, "Her parents already told us about the other boys who were interested in her. One of them probably beat Boyle over the head and then took the McCloskey girl with him."

It was a theory that most of those investigating the case had already considered. Rose's parents *had* informed the police of other young men who had pursued their daughter romantically, but Rose had eyes only for Dennis Boyle. Still, one of these other potential suitors, feeling jealous of Dennis, and angry by Rose's rejection, could have attacked Boyle and then kidnapped the girl. It was possible that Rose McCloskey—perhaps injured, undoubtedly terrified—was being held captive somewhere in the city.

By daybreak on the morning of January 5, 1933, Fairmount Park was teeming with investigators and volunteers, all actively searching for Rose McCloskey. They combed through the park and wandered down little-used paths, breaking through thorny brambles and peering into bushes, desperate to find the missing girl.

Around 6:00 a.m., as police and volunteers cursed the cold and the thickness of the park's vegetation, their search was interrupted by the shrill sound of a whistle being blown. Over and over and over again the piercing whistle broke the silence. Investigators abandoned what they were doing and rushed to follow it.

Three hundred yards from the park's main entrance, officers came upon a panic-stricken guard who seemed unable to stop his incessant whistle blowing. Even as the group of lawmen and volunteers approached, the shrieking peals continued until someone finally pulled the whistle from the man's mouth. He was clearly upset and agitated, trembling and unable to speak, as he gestured frantically towards some large gravel heaps situated behind him.

The gravel towered to a height of nearly 15 feet and was used for maintenance on the park trails. Tentatively, police walked around it and encountered a scene of such gruesome carnage that it stopped them dead in their tracks.

Fifteen yards in front of them lay the body of a young girl sprawled awkwardly beneath a twin catalpa tree. She was frozen in death, her body covered by a thin sheen of frost that seemed to shimmer and sparkle in the early morning sun. She was nude from the waist down, with her dress hiked up around her upper torso which was twisted into a grotesque and unnatural position. Her right hand was clenched in a fist, her head battered, and her hair matted with glistening blood.

Edging closer, the officers were horrified to discover that the girl had been nearly scalped. Deep, penetrating wounds had split the skin of her head, causing the hair to hang loose, flipping and flopping at bizarre and disjointed angles.

Blood saturated the area, so much blood, in fact, that police feared there must be another victim hidden somewhere nearby. It wasn't until they drew closer to the body that the bloodbath was explained. Not only had the girl been viciously beaten, but someone had slashed her throat as well. It was horrifying, shocking, and one of the most disturbing crime scenes any of those investigating had ever seen.

Glancing around, police noticed three park benches sitting directly behind the gravel heaps facing away from them. Although the benches were located a mere 300 yards from the park entrance, they might as well have been 300 *miles* from it. The gravel blocked one's view of the benches and transformed that area of the park into an isolated and secluded place. There was no lighting there, leaving the space in absolute darkness, and from inside the park, the gravel appeared to be the park boundary bordering the street. This explained why no one had found the body the previous night; no one even knew this section of the park existed.

Officers could see that the ground if front of the nearest bench showed evidence of a recent struggle, and looking closer, they found several strands of long, dark hair, matted with blood, clinging to it. There was a blood-trail leading away from the bench, and following it ten feet further on, they discovered a woman's black suede shoe, and shortly thereafter, a woman's tan hat as well. The zigzag trail of blood moved between the gravel heaps, where additional evidence of a struggle was noted, and then meandered through a mud puddle, where the mate to the black suede shoe was recovered. From there, the blood droplets led directly to the girl's dead body.

"She must have been attacked on the bench," one of the officers theorized, as he kneeled near the disturbed gravel, "and then attempted to escape, but she fell as she was trying to get away." The officer tilted his head at an angle, his eyes following the blood-trail, then stood up and pointed farther along. "It looks like she made it over to there," he said, indicating another patch of disrupted gravel, "before falling again."

The other investigators nodded their heads in agreement. The trail of blood wound in and out between smaller mounds of gravel, then zigzagged here and there in no orderly fashion. It looked like someone had been bleeding profusely, and had wandered aimlessly in a daze, much like Dennis Boyle had done.

Curiously though, if this girl *was* Rose McCloskey—and police were fairly certain that it was since no other girl had been reported missing—then how had Dennis Boyle made it so far from the crime scene? Boyle had been discovered nearly three blocks away from the park's entrance; quite a distance to travel for a man so gravely injured.

~*~*~

By noon, the crime scene had been roped off, and the body of the young girl moved to the mortuary. As several detectives remained behind, continuing to gather evidence and interview park guards, a group of five young males sauntered nonchalantly past the scene. The men were young, in their late teens or early twenties, loud, laughing and joking, and obviously obnoxious. Upon reaching the officers, one of them suddenly stopped, hacked up a wad of saliva, and spit right in front of them. Smirking, the youth continued on his way, his companions grinning their approval.

"That's a bad bunch," one of the guards said, his face showing disgust. "That's the group that's been wreaking havoc in the park for months, following women and harassing them."

Furious at the spitting incident and the boys' conduct in general, several officers went after the group and presently returned with the five men in tow. Despite the youths' indignant protests that they had done nothing wrong, each of them were handcuffed and taken down to headquarters.

The police were disgusted by the boys, who were disrespectful, acted like the murder of the young girl was no big deal, and appeared bored and angry by this disruption in their lives. They knew nothing about any murder, they insisted, and demanded to be let go.

Antagonizing the police is never a wise thing to do, and this group of boys had foolishly done just that. Instead of letting them go, the infuriated officers locked each of them in a cell, hoping a few days in jail might teach them a lesson.

Later that same afternoon, Patrick McCloskey positively identified the dead girl from the park as his nineteen-year-old daughter, Rose. It was imperative that the police be able to question Dennis Boyle, but a quick call to the hospital revealed that his condition was unchanged; the man was still in a coma.

A check of recent incident reports, revealed that another young woman, a local seamstress, had been attacked near the park exactly one week earlier. On the previous Wednesday evening, December 29, 1932, Mae Kine* had been walking home from work around 9:00 pm, using a route that took her behind the Rodin Museum and along the main entrance to Fairmount Park. She was alone in the dark—no one was around, and no one was following her—when suddenly she was grabbed from behind and a gloved hand was clamped firmly over her mouth. Mae began to struggle fiercely, and somehow managed to break free from her attacker's grasp. Terrified, she bolted away, screaming at the top of her lungs, and hadn't stopped running until she reached the door of her apartment house. Police were disappointed that she could give them no description of her attacker, but the incident tended to confirm their worst fears and suspicions; whoever the stalker was, his crimes were quickly escalating.

Two days later, on January 7th, Dennis Boyle finally regained consciousness but only for a few brief moments. Police, who had been sitting vigil at his bedside since the attack, leaned closer to hear what the young man had to say. Boyle claimed that he and a "female companion" had been sitting on a bench in Fairmount Park when a dark colored sedan drove up. Two men got out and suddenly attacked them.

"We were only there a short time when I was hit from behind and stunned," the weak man gasped out. "I didn't see our assailants, but I think they were white. That's all I remember."

When the detectives asked him who his companion was, Boyle claimed he didn't know the girl's name. The authorities got the impression that Dennis Boyle believed Rose had escaped the attack and was reluctant to involve her. Because doctors had already warned them not to tell Dennis that Rose had been killed, the officers didn't press him about this. Less than 30 minutes after he awoke, Dennis Boyle lapsed back into a coma, and the interrogation came to an end. Police were grateful to have at least gotten a description of the dark-colored sedan, and the information that two men were involved in the attack.

The next day, January 8, 1933, police finally released the five "hoodlums" they were still holding at the police station. The cocky attitude the boys had arrived with had diminished after spending nearly three days in jail, and most of them thanked the officers when they were let go. One, however, did not; this boy simply glared at the detectives, which didn't surprise them at all. They had found that young man to be a tough case, hard as nails, and someone well on his way to becoming a seasoned criminal. For that reason, they decided to keep the youth under secret surveillance.

~*~*~

The murder of teenage Rose McCloskey stunned Philadelphia and put the entire city on edge. Crime happened, of course, but this type of savage murder, especially of a young girl, was not at all common. Newspapers and the public were demanding that police find the girl's killer and do so quickly, but authorities had few clues to work with. After listening to the brief statement Dennis Boyle had made, Captain Heanley decided to call a press conference to update the public on the investigation.

Facing the media, Heanley's tone was gruff as he began, "From footsteps found at the scene, it appears that at least two people were on top of the gravel heap when the couple sat down. The men apparently jumped from the gravel and landed directly behind the bench. We've found four deep imprints in the gravel which bears this out." Curiously, he made no mention of a dark-colored sedan.

~*~*~

On January 11, 1933, Rose McCloskey was buried in the city of Philadelphia, where more than a hundred people came to pay their respects. Rose's parents were devastated by her death, her mother so grief-stricken that she needed support just to walk. Several detectives mingled with the crowd, looking for anyone who appeared suspicious or out of place.

Later that same afternoon, a city police officer noticed a young, black male—dressed entirely in rags—sneaking into an abandoned brewery located near the entrance to Fairmount Park. The man looked suspicious—furtively glancing over his shoulder, as if to see if anyone were watching—and the officer immediately decided to follow him. Once inside the brewery, it became apparent that the man was actually living in the abandoned building. Even more alarming, the place was strewn with women's clothing, and numerous pictures adorning the cement walls showed nude and risqué females. Taking the man into custody, the officer brought him down to police headquarters where he identified himself as John Goodman, a twenty-five-year-old rag-picker. That was why there were so many clothes strewn around his lodgings, Goodman insisted; they were just rags, that's all. He denied having anything to do with Rose McCloskey's murder, and repeatedly told the officers that he was not a violent man.

Believing that Rose had fought with her attacker, the police decided to check John Goodman's body for injuries. As the man began to undress, the officer's watched in stunned silence. Piece by piece, as John Goodman shed his tattered outerwear, it was discovered that he was completely attired in women's clothing underneath: dress, silk panties, and sheer stockings. John Goodman looked highly embarrassed and quickly denied that he enjoyed dressing in this way. He told the investigators that he did so only to keep warm; he owned no coat. The officers were skeptical. Pressed further, Goodman finally admitted that he also liked the way women's clothing felt on him.

Although the rag-picker was strange, and it was discovered that he had a prior record for a non-violent crime, police could find no connection between him and the attack in Fairmount Park. They had no choice but to reluctantly let their suspect go.

That same evening, Detective Joseph Lestrango called another press conference to tell the public that "eight or nine men were involved in the attack, not two as previously stated." He declined to offer any reason for this new theory, and refused to elaborate on what had caused the investigation to shift so drastically. Apparently, police had no idea how many people were involved in the attack, or what had actually happened to Dennis Boyle and Rose McCloskey. But the twists and turns the case seemed to take so often, continued.

The next day, January 12th, authorities got a visit from the three youths who had brought Dennis Boyle to the hospital. They hadn't mentioned it previously, the boys told the investigators, but when they found Dennis Boyle he had been mumbling to himself, and they distinctly heard him say, "I had a fight with Jim."

Police thought it unusual that the boys hadn't revealed this from the start, and they weren't sure whether to believe the statement or not. The case was becoming a nightmare, and authorities were frustrated. They had been stopping dark-colored sedans all over the city. Some were looking for eight or nine different men, and now they'd have to track down everyone they could find named Jim.

"Jesus Christ," one of the officer's mumbled in disgust, "What's next?"

Slowly, Dennis Boyle's condition began to improve. He had regained consciousness several times, but only for brief periods, and had finally abandoned his tale of not knowing the name of his female companion. He often asked about Rose, and it was clear that he no longer believed his fiancé had escaped the attack. Knowing, though, that he was not out of the woods yet, no one told him that she was dead for fear that the news might impede his recovery.

Two days after telling the public that eight or nine men were involved in the attack, police changed their story once again. Now they told the press that the killer was "a lone, extremely powerful lunatic who had a passion for bludgeoning 'petters'."

In fact, this new theory was not so new after all. It had actually come about shortly after Rose's body was found, when a Philadelphia police officer made the comment that the crime looked a lot like the work of 8-X, an unknown predator who had preyed on roadside couples in New York several years earlier. The press had dubbed the killer 8-X for unknown reasons, and the case had never been solved.

Philadelphia officials contacted Inspector Harold King of Nassau County, New York, and inquired about any information—or a description of—the mysterious 8-X. King, who had been frustrated by his failure to capture the elusive predator was excited to get the inquiry, but as soon as he read the description of the Philadelphia attack he realized that it bore no resemblance to the crimes of 8-X. Interestingly enough, however, it did bear a striking similarity to an unsolved case he was working on right then.

The crime that King was thinking about was already eight months old and cold, but it had been vicious in its brutality and had left Nassau detectives frustrated that they had not been able to solve it. It involved the murder of thirty-two-year-old Edward Brinker, a married man with a young daughter from Jackson Heights, Long Island, and thirty-year-old Rose Welk, a single girl who hailed from Flushing, Queens.

On April 20, 1932, the battered bodies of Brinker and Welk had been found lying in a vacant lot in Williston Park, two miles north of Mineola, Long Island. Brinker had been severely bludgeoned and stabbed in the chest and the throat. Twenty-five feet away lay Rose Welk, her head bashed to a pulp and her mouth taped, but incredibly, still alive. The vacant lot showed evidence of a terrific struggle, and Edward Brinker's car, which the couple had driven earlier that evening, was nowhere to be found.

As police worked the scene, word came from the hospital that Rose Welk had been pronounced DOA, and had never regained consciousness. The next day, Brinker's car was found abandoned in Bayside, the interior splattered with drying blood. Police assumed the killer had used the vehicle for his getaway, and hoped he lived somewhere in the vicinity where it was found.

There had been little progress made in the case, however, and when Inspector King heard about the McCloskey/Boyle attack in Philadelphia, the similarities had immediately piqued his interest. Each female victim was named Rose, each crime was committed against lovers "parking" in isolated locations, each was committed at the same time of night, and when the moon was in the same phase of fullness. Both deceased victims at the scene—Brinker in New York and McCloskey in Pennsylvania—had received a total of nine skull fractures, while each of those who initially survived the attack—Boyle in Pennsylvania and Welk in New York—had received a total of three. There appeared to be no motive for either crime, no rape or robbery involved, and when King looked at the pictures of Rose McCloskey lying under the twin catalpa tree in Fairmount Park, he felt the hair on the back of his neck stand on end. Rose McCloskey's body had been posed in the same grotesque position as Rose Welk's. King was so intrigued by these similarities, that on January 8, 1933, he secretly sent one of his officers, Detective Sergeant Marcel Chagnon, to Philadelphia to investigate.

~*~*~

By January 14th, Dennis Boyle was waking for longer periods of time and realized that his fiancé was never there when he did. He was concerned about that, and almost afraid to ask, but finally decided he had to.

"Is Rose dead?" Dennis suddenly asked his police protector.

Caught off guard by the question, the officer was unsure of what to say. He knew that doctors still feared what the shock of Rose's death might do to their patient, so rather than tell him the truth, he decided to give him a hint.

"We won't talk about that right now," the officer told the worried patient, "but I will tell you she's much worse off than you are."

Dennis nodded, understanding what he had already feared. The officer didn't have to come right out and tell him, he knew; if Rose was "much worse off" than himself, the chances were pretty good that she had not survived. Dennis mulled it over in his mind for a moment and then suddenly spoke again. "We were attacked by a gang of hoodlums who I couldn't see," Dennis said, turning to look at the detective. Then, as if just remembering about it, Dennis asked eagerly, "Did the other couple see anything?"

The officer looked surprised. "What other couple?" he asked.

"There was another couple in the park that night, sitting on a bench about fifty yards away," Dennis said. "They must have seen the attack."

The officer shrugged his shoulders and told Dennis he didn't know anything about it, but he immediately relayed the information back to headquarters. No one in authority had heard anything about another couple being near the scene that night, and they wondered why, with all the appeals for help they had relayed to the public, no one had come forward to tell about it. Of course, who knew if Dennis Boyle was telling the truth, or even if he had any real memory of the attack? This was the third version he had provided, and none of them had led anywhere.

~*~*~

On January 24th, Philadelphia police announced the arrest of twenty-seven-year-old Earl Morris on a charge of "suspicion" in the death of Rose McCloskey, and the attempted murder of Dennis Boyle. The frightened residents of the city gave a sigh of relief at the news and immediately began to relax.

They should not have. What no one in the public realized was that the police had arrested the man on nothing more than a tip: a claim that he never left his mother's home until after dark. That was it, nothing more. By the next day, the police admitted as much to reporters, stating that they had "absolutely nothing to connect him to the murder." Despite this admission, however, they refused to release Morris, and held him for almost four entire days on a simple charge of "suspicion." It seemed that the police were so desperate to solve the crime that they were reluctant to let a person go even after they had cleared him.

By the beginning of February, Dennis Boyle was well on his way to recovery, but he was unable to walk and needed to get around with a wheelchair. Doctors had assured his worried family that this was only temporary and that Dennis would one day walk again.

On February 14, 1933, Boyle was finally released from the hospital, but he was not allowed to go home and celebrate. Instead, detectives drove him directly down to police headquarters where they subjected him to a grueling interrogation that lasted nearly 48 hours. Nothing new was revealed through the questioning, however, and the murder of Rose McCloskey appeared well on its way to the unsolved file.

As the temperature began to rise and winter moved into spring, police continued to hunt for the killer of Rose McCloskey, but they made little progress with the case. They hauled countless suspects into police headquarters, holding some and releasing others, and they continued to keep a close eye on the group of "hoodlums" who were still wreaking havoc in Fairmount Park.

The McCloskey/Boyle case was no longer front page news, and by summer, it seemed that most people in the city had forgotten about it. The police, however, had not forgotten. Although the investigation might have come to a halt, the murder of Rose McCloskey ate away at them, and they remained determined to find her killer no matter how long it took.

~*~*~

On June 12, 1933, more than five months after the attack on Rose McCloskey and Dennis Boyle, an elderly gentleman entered the Philadelphia police station and stood awkwardly just inside the door. He kept his eyes riveted to the floor, only occasionally glancing up to look shyly around the busy precinct. After a short time, an officer approached the man and asked if he could help him.

The man seemed almost relieved by the offer and told the detective that he wanted to talk to someone about the "murder in Fairmount Park."
"The Rose McCloskey case?" the officer immediately asked, to which the older man nodded his head.

The man was taken into Captain Harry Heanley's office where he identified himself as Thomas Barry, age sixty-six, and stated he was employed as a trolley car crossing watchman. "I'm here," Barry began quietly, "because I was in the park the night that little girl was killed."

Heanley felt his heart skip a beat. Barry looked scared, haunted, and utterly sincere. Could the police finally be getting the break they had waited more than five months for?

"Go on," the captain urged, leaning forward on his desk.

Thomas Barry shook his head slightly, and then looked at the police captain, his face radiating shame. "I know I should have come here a lot sooner," he cried, "but I was so afraid of those thugs who roamed the park."
"It's okay," the captain soothed, anxious to hear what the man had to say. "You're here now."

"This has tortured me for the past five months," Barry announced, his voice dropping to a whisper. "I tried to forget about it, but she won't let me. And when Rose told me I had to tell you what I knew, well . . . I knew I had to come."

"Rose who?" Heanley asked.

"Rose McCloskey," Barry answered, seeming surprised that the detective didn't know who he meant.

Captain Heanley slowly leaned back in his chair, his excitement waning. *Rose McCloskey told Thomas to tell what he knew?* Heanley thought to himself. *What kind of nut do I have here?* But he kept his disappointment hidden, and asked the older man to continue.

"Well, me and my girl were in the park that night, when a man began to follow us," Barry said. "He scared us both, and we tried to hurry along. There was another couple there, too, and as I urged my girl along, this man stopped following us and began following the other couple. Just a few minutes later we heard screaming, and quickly left the park."

Barry looked up at the silent detective before continuing. "I wanted to come and tell you sooner, but I was just so afraid. Rose has been coming to me in my dreams and telling me I have to tell. I ignored her until last night when I woke up and she was standing right in front of me. It wasn't a dream; I wasn't sleeping. Rose McCloskey was standing right there at the foot my bed. She was beaten up, and covered with blood, and she looked so sad that it broke my heart. She pleaded with me to help find her killer by telling the police what I know."

Heanley didn't believe in ghosts and spirits, but the man's story did corroborate what Dennis Boyle had said about another couple being in the park at the time of the attack, and he needed to know if Barry had actually been in the park that night. Choosing to ignore the supernatural element of his story, Heanley instead asked Barry if he would be able to recognize the man who had followed

Barry answered immediately, nodding his head. "He's one of that group of thugs who are always bothering people in the park. You can't miss the guy; he's almost seven feet tall."

Heanley's breath caught for a moment, and he felt a surge of excitement course through his veins. Seven feet tall, he thought? He knew exactly who Thomas Barry was talking about; twenty-three-year-old Richard "Big Slim" Bach.

Bach was, indeed, a rough character, and had been among the five hoodlums initially picked up within days of the murder. He had also been the one that officers had placed under secret surveillance at that time. Bach hadn't said anything to connect him with the murder while in jail; there was just something about the youth that nagged at the officers and caused them to conduct surveillance on him once he was released.

Since police had been keeping watch over him, they had seen Bach return to the park on several occasions and accost young couples there, but he had never done anything that would warrant his arrest. To the police, Bach appeared to be little more than a big, immature bully, not a violent criminal.

Now, however, with the information provided by Thomas Barry, Heanley ordered two of his detectives to secretly search their new suspect's room. In 1933, neither search warrants nor permission was required, and unbeknown to Bach, the officers entered his premises undetected, and rifled through his belongings. They returned to the precinct shortly, obviously excited, and carrying a sealed paper bag containing a heavy hunting knife sporting an 8 inch serrated blade. Near the hilt, clearly visible, were traces of a substance that might have been dried blood.

On June 14, 1933 police arrested Richard Bach at the home of his mother, Josephine, and took him down to the station. There he was forced to participate in a line-up, viewed by both Thomas Barry and Dennis Boyle. Barry immediately picked Bach out as the youth who had followed him and his girlfriend on the night in question, but Boyle just shook his head. He had never gotten a look at his attacker, he said, and couldn't identify Bach.

After the line-up, Bach was subjected to a grueling interrogation that lasted most of the day and into the night, but he repeatedly denied any involvement in the crime. He didn't kill Rose McCloskey, he insisted, and hadn't been anywhere near Fairmount Park that night. He had never seen Dennis Boyle before, or Thomas Barry, and if they said he was there that night, then they were lying.Police didn't believe him, and they badgered their prisoner, getting right in his face, slamming their fists upon the table, and repeatedly calling him a liar. Around 4:00 am in the morning, Richard Bach suddenly slumped back in his chair, covered his face with his hands, and began to cry. Weakly, he whispered, "Okay. I did it."

Surprised, Captain Heanley sat up straighter in his chair. "Excuse me?" he asked.

Richard Bach raised his eyes to meet the detectives, and said simply, "I did it. I killed her."

More coffee was called for, as well as cigarettes, and then each of the men in the little interrogation room settled back to hear what Richard Bach had to say.

~*~*~

The police wasted no time alerting the press to the fact that they had "solved" the McCloskey case, and even before their suspect had completed his confession, the media, in turn, had informed Rose's parents. Upon hearing that Richard Bach had confessed to the murder of their daughter, Annie and Patrick McCloskey each gave statements to the press.

Patrick seemed very pleased with the news, saying with a smile, "I'm tickled to death. Now maybe I'll be able to sleep at night."

Annie, however, was angry, as she told the reporters, "I hope he goes to the electric chair! It's too bad the law won't allow him to die in the same terrible way my daughter died."

Later that afternoon, June 15, 1933, Richard Bach was taken to Fairmount Park where he agreed to re-enact the attack he perpetrated on Dennis Boyle and Rose McCloskey. While at the police station giving his confession, the prisoner had appeared morose and remorseful, but by the time he arrived at the crime scene Richard Bach was almost giddy, and clearly enjoying the attention. Police had brought along a dummy to pose as Rose, and Bach pointed to a bench—the same bench where police had found strands of bloody hair—to indicate where Rose had been sitting and where police should place it.

"The couple was embracing when I saw them," Bach began, "and I don't know why it is, but whenever I see a woman in a man's arms, I lose control of myself." The sight of Rose in Dennis Boyle's arms had both enraged and excited him, Bach said, and he had climbed the fifteen foot-high gravel pile behind the couple, intent on attacking them.

At this point, Bach grinned broadly and scurried up the gravel. After reaching the top, he stared down at the bench below him where the dummy of Rose had been placed. "I picked up a large rock," he called down to his captors, "that must have weighed between four and five pounds, and heaved it down towards the bench. When I threw the rock," he continued, "it hit the man in the head, and then I ran down the hill and grabbed the girl."

Bach demonstrated his actions by scurrying back down the gravel pit and grabbing the dummy from the bench. But, he told the investigators; the girl had started to struggle, fighting and screaming, so he punched her in the face causing her nose and mouth to erupt in a geyser of blood.

Bach was gripping the dummy by the shoulder as he viciously hit it in the face to demonstrate, using enough force to nearly rip the head free of the body.

"I dragged her to a tree," he said as he began lugging the mock girl towards the twin catalpa, "but she continued to fight, so I picked up a rock and hit her again."

He dropped the dummy to the ground and fell to his knees, leaning over it and holding an imaginary rock in his upraised hand. Over and over and over again, Richard Bach brought his arm up and down, slamming it into the dummy's head, demonstrating what he had done to Rose McCloskey's skull.

"I realized then that I had hurt her badly," he said, "and I panicked. I knew she would die, but she was suffering, and I wanted to end it. So that's when I slashed her throat." Afterwards, Bach said, he had quickly fled, hurrying home where he went straight to bed.

Bach made no mention of the girl having escaped, nor did he give any explanation for the signs of a struggle, or the zigzag trail of blood between the gravel heaps. He also didn't bother to explain how Rose's shoes ended up yards away from each other, and even farther from her body. The officers, however, didn't question him about this, nor did they care. They had a confession—one that would send Richard Bach straight to Rockview State Prison and Pennsylvania's "Old Smokey" electric chair—and that was all they needed.

~*~*~

News spread quickly that the police had finally made an arrest in the Rose McCloskey case—and had secured a confession to boot—and the papers scrambled to interview anyone who had a connection with the young killer. Due to his size, and much to Bach's annoyance, the press quickly dubbed him "The Giant Murderer."

Richard Bach was born in 1910, to exceedingly poor and destitute parents. Sickly as a child, he was rarely taken to the doctor, simply because his parents couldn't afford to treat the many ailments their young son seemed to pick up. Instead, his mother would care for him at home, where he was kept isolated in his bedroom, and not allowed out of bed. As a consequence, little Richard missed a lot of school and made few friends.

By the time the boy reached his early teens he had fallen way behind those his own age academically. He was humiliated and embarrassed to see children much younger than himself mastering schoolwork he couldn't understand, and those same children often teased and ridiculed him for being both slow—which he wasn't—and for his size. Richard Bach seemed to just grow, and grow and grow, reaching a height of 6-feet 7-inches by the age of sixteen. He towered over classmates and teachers alike, and was forced to endure the silly one-liners everyone—except himself—thought so funny such as, "Hey, how's the weather up there?." Girls his own age looked at him like he was a pariah, and he quickly discovered that they wanted nothing to do with him.

Had Richard chose to channel his frustrations on the basketball court, he might have become one of America's all time star players, but he didn't view his abnormal physique as a gift. Instead, he considered it a curse, and thought of himself as a freak of nature. He finally quit school—and what he termed "the constant abuse" he endured there—at the age of sixteen, and soon became sullen and withdrawn. He was ashamed of his height, and embarrassed to be seen in public, instead secreting himself at home during the day and venturing out only at night.

It wasn't long before Richard began meeting up with other "outcasts," and running with a bad crowd who seemed to delight in wreaking havoc among the young lovers in Fairmount Park. Richard's mother, Josephine, had coddled the boy when he was young and often ill, and later found that she had little control over him. Still, she tried to help, and demanded that her son get a job, which Richard did—in fact he got several—but he was never able to hold on to any of them. Soon, those who knew him were using words like "no-good," and "problem child" to describe him, and few had trouble believing he was responsible for the brutal crime he was now charged with.

Josephine Bach, however, didn't think so. She knew her son had problems, but she couldn't believe he was a cold-blooded murderer. That was too much for any mother to accept. She had been upset by the statements the McCloskey's gave the newspapers—especially Annie McCloskey, who appeared so anxious to see her son sit in the electric chair—and Josephine spoke to reporters herself. She sobbed as she exclaimed, "My boy is innocent! We were playing cards together when the murder occurred. I was sick and sat up in bed propped up by pillows playing cards with him. He was sick too." Josephine appeared sincere as she protested her son's innocence, but few people believed her tale.

~*~*~

Richard Bach was transferred to the southern part of Philadelphia, and housed in Moyamensing Prison: a massive, Goth-like structure constructed almost entirely of brick and stone, and sporting turrets and towers like some medieval castle. The prison had housed its fair share of notorious people, including Edgar Allen Poe, who spent a night there, and the infamous serial killer, H. H. Holmes, who was hanged there in 1896.

On June 16, Bach was taken out of Moyamensing and brought before the court for a secret arraignment where attorney Harry H. Johns was appointed to defend him. The youth was ordered to be held without bail until the grand jury convened on June 20th, at which time the District Attorney would ask for indictments against him on charges of murder and manslaughter.

On June 22, Dennis Boyle and Walter Petry, Sergeant of Park Guards at Fairmount Park, testified before the grand jury which immediately handed down three true bills against Richard "Big Slim" Bach. "The Giant Murderer" was indicted on one count of first-degree murder, one count of voluntary and involuntary manslaughter and one count of assault and battery with intent to kill. He was formally arraigned the next day in Quarter Sessions Court in Philadelphia before Judge Horace Stern, where he pled not guilty.

The trial of Richard Bach for the murder of Rose McCloskey and the attempted murder of Dennis Boyle began on July 18, 1933, before the Honorable Judge Harry S. McDevitt. Bach sat at the defense table looking sullen and bored, his long legs splayed beneath the table because his knees wouldn't fit if he bent them.

The first witness to take the stand was Patrick McCloskey, who told about his and his wife's growing panic when Rose failed to return home that bitter January night, and then learning that Dennis Boyle was in the hospital and not expected to live. It was at that point, Patrick admitted, that he knew something terrible had happened to his daughter, and his fear had turned to dread. Breaking into sobs, the grief-stricken man went on to testify about the devastating job of identifying the girl's battered corpse the next day.

Dennis Boyle was the next witness to take the stand. He had still not fully recovered from his injuries, and although he was finally out of his wheelchair, he walked with a pronounced limp, clear evidence of the beating he had sustained. As he took his seat, he shifted his eyes to the defense table, and leveled a glare at Richard Bach that was so intense the courtroom guard moved a step closer to the prisoner. Bach, however, looking gangly and bored at the defense table, refused to meet the witness's gaze.

Boyle had little to say, telling the jury, "I was talking and Rose was listening and then everything went black. The next thing I knew, I was in a hospital, and later they told me that Rose was dead."

By far the most interesting witness was Thomas Barry, the trolley car crossing guard who had been in the park on the night of the murder. Barry testified to the agony he had endured while keeping his secret for five full months, and to Rose haunting his dreams each night. When he testified about her ghostly visit that last night, he did so honestly and sincerely. "No," he said adamantly, "it was not a dream. It was Rose's ghost standing before me."

By the next day, the District Attorney was already wrapping up his case. After reading Richard Bach's confession to the jury, the prosecution rested.

Defense attorney Harry Johns rose to address the jury and, mocking Thomas Barry, told them not to be swayed by stories of "ghosts and apparitions." He would put his client on the stand, he said, to recant his confession, and offer up an alibi witness for the time of the crime. "Richard Bach did not kill Rose McCloskey," Johns thundered, adding that his client was not even in Fairmount Park the night she died.

Rising to take the stand, Richard Bach towered over everyone else in the courtroom. Vehemently denying that he had killed the dead girl and assaulted her boyfriend, Bach claimed that he had confessed only out of fear of the police. "I didn't do it," he cried. "I was with my mother that entire night."

Josephine Bach, the alibi witness that Harry Johns had promised, also took the stand to relate the story of her and her son playing cards at the time of the murder. Once Josephine left the stand, Johns stood as if to call his next witness, but instead, simply said, "The defense rests."

Incredibly, it was over. Those in the courtroom appeared stunned and aghast. Johns had put on only two witnesses, and in their opinion, had put on no defense at all.

Judge McDevitt decided to postpone closing arguments and give the jury of twelve men the night off, instructing them to report to court early the next day, July 21, 1933.

The next day, after scant closing arguments by both sides, the jury was handed the case and went out to deliberate Richard Bach's fate. Exactly one hour later they were back.

The defendant was told to stand and did so, keeping his eyes glued to the table and remaining unemotional and quiet as the foreman read the verdict of "guilty of murder in the first degree," with a recommendation that the defendant be sentenced to death.

Judge McDevitt thanked the jury for their service, and then postponed sentencing pending an appeal by Bach's attorney. Harry Johns immediately filed a motion for a new trial, but he knew that barring the verdict being overturned, the "Giant Murderer" was headed for Rockview State Penitentiary, and Pennsylvania's "Old Smokey" electric chair.

~*~*~

On September 8, 1933, Richard Bach appeared with his attorney before three judges—Harry McDevitt, Albert Miller, and George Parry—in Common Pleas Court in the heart of Philadelphia. There, Harry Johns argued that the jury's verdict and the death sentence leveled against his client went against the weight of the evidence.

The panel of judges took the argument under advisement and scheduled a hearing for September 15th, at which time they would hand down their decision.

On September 13th, Richard Bach contacted his attorney and told him he desperately needed to see him. When they were together in the jail visiting room, Bach suddenly turned to Harry Johns and blurted out; "You know, I didn't kill that girl, but I was there."

Johns remained quiet and waited for him to continue.

"I was only a lookout," Bach insisted, "and I had no idea he was actually going to kill her."

"You had no idea who was going to kill her?" Johns asked.

Bach hesitated for a moment before telling his attorney that the real killer of Rose McCloskey was a man named John Phillips, who lived at 40th Street near Poplar. According to Bach, Phillips was only supposed to mug the couple while he kept watch, but when the mugging "went bad," and turned into an all-out assault, Bach claimed he had gotten scared and fled the scene. He added that he hadn't wanted to say anything because he didn't want people to think he was a "rat."

Great, Harry Johns thought, *just great*. The judges were scheduled to hand down their decision on Bach's appeal in only two days, and now his client was providing him with an entirely new scenario of the crime. Johns didn't know if the youth's story was true, but it intrigued him. He knew that Rose's body had been found at 40th and Girard Avenue, very near to where Bach said the real killer lived, and, what's more, Harry Johns was already familiar with the name John Phillips.

Although he had never represented Phillips, he had heard a lot about the man and knew him to be a rough character who had been charged with a number of crimes in the past, including assault and robbery.

Harry Johns found himself in a dilemma. Bach's hearing was only two days away, and there wouldn't be enough time to investigate his allegations. So, claiming that he was working on new evidence that would prove his client's innocence, Johns immediately filed a motion to delay the judge's decision, and was relieved when the court agreed to a one-week stay.

Rather than confer with police to verify whether Phillips might be a viable suspect in Rose McCloskey's murder, Johns decided to keep his new information a secret, electing to go for the element of surprise instead. When he and his client arrived at City Hall on September 22, 1933, and made their way to Room 453 of Quarter Sessions Court, Johns had no way of knowing that he was about to get the surprise of a lifetime.

Ignorance is bliss, so they say, and as Johns stood and began arguing that it wasn't Richard Bach who had killed Rose McCloskey, but an ex-con named John Phillips, the door to the courtroom suddenly flew open and two men walked inside. One of them was William J. Connelly, chief of the county detectives, and the other was obviously a prisoner, dressed in prison garb and being held by the upper arm as the detective escorted him in.

The prisoner was walked directly in front of the three panel judge and asked to identify himself.

"John Phillips," the man answered icily.

"And where do you reside?"

"Western State Penitentiary," the man replied, turning to glare at Richard Bach, who refused to meet his gaze.

"And how long have you been in prison sir?"

"I was convicted of false-pretense in March of 1932 and sentenced to two years."

March of 1932; almost an entire year before Rose McCloskey was murdered. The room erupted into gasps and snickers, and Harry Johns, deeply embarrassed, visibly blanched. Though he had no way of knowing it, the conversation at the county jail between him and Richard Bach had been overheard by a jailer who had immediately informed the police.

Knowing there was no possible way Phillips could be responsible for the crime, one of the judges leaned over the bench, looked past Johns, and to the defendant. "Do you have anything to say, Mr. Bach?" the judge asked sarcastically.

Richard Bach, looking embarrassed himself, mumbled that he wanted to recant his confession regarding John Phillips' guilt, but he had nothing else to say. Looking disgusted, Judge McDevitt, who had presided over Bach's original trial, quickly denied his appeal.

As Bach sat with his hand pressed against his forehead and a sullen look on his face, McDevitt asked if he had anything to say before they passed sentence.

Richard immediately dropped his hand, sat straighter in his chair, and looked squarely at the judge. "Go ahead," he said angrily.

The panel of three judges sentenced the youth to die in Pennsylvania's electric chair at Rockview State Penitentiary, telling him that Governor Gifford Pinchot would set his execution date shortly.

In the back of the courtroom, a heart-wrenching wail erupted, and everyone turned to see Josephine Bach, who was sobbing and crying, rise from her seat. The woman looked devastated and panicked, like a terrified animal caught in a trap from which there was no escape. She seemed, at first, to try and make her way towards her son, but then abruptly turned and bolted towards the courtroom doors. Suddenly, however, she stopped short, began to swoon, and then collapsed in a heap on the courthouse floor.

Taken into the judge's chambers, Josephine was sufficiently revived in time to visit with her condemned son. Afterwards, Bach was escorted back to the county jail to await transfer to the state penitentiary.

Despite the fact that Harry Johns was furious at his client for humiliating him before the entire court, he was still desperate to save Richard's life, and vowed to appeal to the State Supreme Court and the State Pardon's Board.

Richard Bach's appeals dragged on until early 1934 when the State Supreme Court upheld the young man's murder conviction, and Governor Pinchot set his date with death for March 26, 1934. Bach, however, would have one more chance to escape the executioner when the State Parole Board agreed to hear his petition on March 21, only five days before his scheduled date with death.

The district attorney told the board that not only had Bach confessed to the police, but after his conviction he had confessed the killing to his mother as well. He noted that Josephine was not in the courtroom to deny the accusation, claiming that that in itself was proof that the statement was true.

The defense had very little to work with, calling only one witness, a friend of Bach's by the name of Alice May Thompson.

Thompson testified that Bach had always maintained his innocence to her, and had also admitted that he knew who the real killer was. The only reason Bach refused to tell authorities the true killer's name, Thompson continued, was for fear of being known as a "rat."

The parole board quickly denied Bach's request for a reduction in sentence and refused to interfere with the doomed man's execution. They ordered his immediate transfer to Rockview State Penitentiary's death row.

Johns next appealed to Governor Pinchot for a stay of execution, and, surprisingly, he received one. Bach's new date with death would be on April 9, 1934. Pinchot, however, did not grant the stay out of compassion for Johns or Bach, but simply because Rockview was undergoing a change in personnel at the time.

On March 23, 1934, W.J. McFarland resigned as Deputy Warden of Rockview after having held the position for eight years. Clarence C. Rhoades, former Captain of the Guards, replaced McFarland, and C.D. Johnson became the new Captain of the Guards. It would be Warden Rhoades and C.D. Johnson who would preside over Bach's execution.

McFarland had been a good warden at the prison, but he had come under fierce criticism for his handling of death row prisoners. Despite the fact that he had arranged more than 12 executions while he was acting warden, he had never been comfortable with carrying out death sentences, and had never witnessed an execution himself. McFarland had always preferred to leave the death chamber after making his required personal check of the room, and certainly before the condemned prisoner was brought in and led to the chair. Clarence Rhoads and C.D. Johnson had no qualms about carrying out their jobs, and it would be they who would be in charge of Bach's execution.

On April 6th, Harry Johns petitioned the Governor for a stay of execution on Richard Bach's behalf, but Pinchot denied the request and two days later Bach was transferred from Moyamensing Prison to Rockview. He was housed in one of the death cells only feet from the electric chair and spent the majority of the day closeted in his cell with the prison chaplain, Reverend C.F. Lauer. The night before his execution, Bach slept fitfully when he dozed off at all, which wasn't very often.

On the scheduled day of his death, April 9, 1934, Bach awoke in a foul mood, speaking to no one and refusing breakfast, although he did accept a cup of coffee. Both his head and his right leg were shaved in anticipation of the soon-to-be-attached electrodes, and at 6:45 am, he was walked to the death chamber accompanied by Rhoades, Johnson, and Reverend Lauer, who read passages from the Bible as they walked.

Although Bach remained calm, Doctor J.B. Triestly, who was on hand to pronounce him dead when the time came, later described Bach's appearance as "ghastly white" when they strapped him into the chair.

At 7:01 a.m., 2000 volts of electricity went coursing through the "Giant Murderers'" body, and three minutes later he was pronounced dead.

Richard Bach's death finally brought an end to the Rose McCloskey case, all because the murdered girl's ghost would not rest until justice was done.

Postscript:

Although Richard Bach remained a suspect in the deaths of Helen Loftus and Maurice Scott, he was never charged with their murders. I was unable to discover any conclusion to that particular case, or to the murders of Rose Welk and Edward Brinker in New York. Whether either of these crimes was ever solved remains unknown.

WHAT HAPPENED TO HARRIET KEIM?

(Herrick, PA. The disappearance of Harriet Keim)

Authors note:

Just as this book was ready to go to print, an incident occurred which affected a family I know personally. Harriet Keim, an eighty-four-year-old wife, mother and Grandmother simply vanished from her home without a trace. As days passed, and nothing was found or heard from her, I received a phone call from a friend of the Keims asking if I might consider writing about the case. Since I was just about to publish a book with four separate stories, I offered to include a short piece about her disappearance; a plea for help for Harriet.

Although the following story is different from the ones you've just read, I wanted to do something to help this family. They are good people, who are living in a nightmare of the unknown. Should anyone have seen Harriet Keim, or have any information regarding her disappearance, please call 911 and report it.

One would be hard-pressed to find a more devoted couple than Bill and Harriet Keim. Married since December 31, 1949—nearly sixty-five years—Bill was a Navy career man, and Harriet a loving mother to their two daughters, Sandi and Debby. In 1978, with their children grown, Bill and Harriet decided to retire to the small town of Herrick, Pennsylvania, located twenty-miles north of the city of Scranton.

Herrick, which has since been incorporated into the nearby town of Union Dale, is beautiful country. Surrounded by mountains, the terrain is mostly wooded and covered by lush vegetation so dense it's hard to make your way through it. In summer, it's a green haven, in fall, a spectacular oasis of vivid color, and in winter, a blustery, cold and snowy place. Water is plentiful in the area—ponds, streams, rivers and lakes—and wildlife abundant. The locals have long learned to tolerate sharing their land with bobcats, coyotes, deer and black bear. Hunting is popular there, and so is biking, fishing, swimming and skiing.

The Keims have lived in Herrick for thirty-five years and are a well-liked and well-known couple. Up until two years ago they ran a "Pick-Your-Own" blueberry patch located on the desolate dirt road where they live. They are a normal and typical family just like everyone else; an elderly couple living out their golden years in a small, rural town.

And Herrick is small. Even with its incorporation into Union Dale, the two towns have a combined population of only 300 people. Which is why it was so shocking and bizarre when Harriet Keim simply disappeared without a trace on the morning of September 30, 2014.

~*~*~

It all began on Sunday, September 28, 2014 when Bill Keim had a dizzy spell at church. Fearing he might be having a heart attack, an ambulance was immediately summoned and rushed the man to Geisinger Hospital in the city of Scranton. Bill's eighty-four-year-old wife, Harriet, rode with him in the ambulance, and the Keim's two daughters were quickly notified.

By chance, one of those daughters, Debby, was scheduled to arrive in Pennsylvania that day for a visit. Debby would be traveling from her home in Maryland and was already packed and ready to go when she got the call. Arriving at the hospital later that afternoon, Debby met with her mother and learned, thankfully, that her father had not suffered a heart attack. Doctors, however, still wanted to admit Bill for observation, and Debby and Harriet stayed with him until around 7:00 pm when they left for home. The two women stopped at a Burger King for something to eat, and arrived back in Herrick somewhere between 8:30 and 9:00 pm.

Once inside the house, Harriet began asking Debby where Bill was.

"Don't you remember?" Debby said patiently. "He's in the hospital. You rode there with him in the ambulance from church."

Harriet, however, didn't seem to remember any of that, which didn't surprise her daughter. Debby knew that her mother suffered from dementia, a disease that affected her memory, and the family was used to her forgetting things. Sometimes, Harriet could have a conversation with someone for an hour or more, and not recall anything that was said thirty minutes later. Other than the memory problems, however, the elderly woman was in fairly good health for her age.

Debby awoke early the next morning, Monday, September 29, and took her dog outside, having brought the animal with her from Maryland. Returning to the house she then got her mother up and helped her take her medicine. Harriet was prescribed several drugs which she took daily, including an anti-seizure medication, and Bill had already given instructions to Debby the day before as to what his wife needed to take. The two women then drove to a nearby diner for breakfast then proceeded to the hospital where they arrived sometime between 10:30 and 11:00 am.

Bill was scheduled for several tests that day, and the two women stayed with him until around 3:00 pm when Debby started thinking about her dog being cooped up inside her parents' house. Deciding she should return home to let her out, Debby gave her mother a choice; did Harriet want to stay at the hospital with Bill, or did she want to ride home with Debby and then come back? Harriet, as her daughter knew she would, chose to stay with her husband.

Debby drove back up to Herrick and took care of some chores—feeding the dog, letting her out, emptying the garbage—and then returned to the hospital around 7:00 pm. She visited with her father for about an hour before she and her mother left for home, once again stopping at Burger King for something to eat.

Unlike the previous night, when the two women returned home Monday, Harriet had trouble settling down. She seemed confused and anxious as she repeatedly asked her daughter where Bill was. Debby thought it might be helpful if she wrote everything down for her mother; what had happened, what they did, and what times they left the house and returned. While she worked on that, Harriet went into the bedroom and changed into a pair of red-striped pajamas.

Afterwards, with the hour growing late and Harriet still unable to relax, Debby suggested she come into bed with her. Harriet did so, and as the two women lay in bed, Debby began to read from the notes she had just written. Harriet seemed to listen to what Debby was saying, and appeared to settle down somewhat.

It had been a long day, and Debby was tired. The last thing she recalls seeing that night is the clock, which read 12:52 am, and her mother leaving the bedroom and closing the door. Debby's dog was sleeping in the room, and Harriet always kept the door closed when the dog was there.

Debby awoke around 6:00 am and used the bathroom across from her bedroom. When she came out, Harriet was walking towards her own room, and the two passed in the hall. At that point, Harriet commented that she couldn't sleep, and Debby got the impression that her mother hadn't slept the entire night. Debby went back to her own room and dozed off again awaking for the second time at 7:30, only to find that her mother wasn't there.

Though concerned, Debby wasn't initially afraid and expected to find her mother at any moment. But as she searched the house and the loft with no sign of her, and then the garage and the yard with the same result, Debby began to get scared. Where was her mother?

She knew Harriet had been confused the night before, and wondered if she might have gone out to look for Bill. It was a foggy morning, and Debby realized that if her mother had wandered off she might not be able to get back home. Quickly, she hopped in her Jeep and drove to the end of the road, but she saw nothing and no one. Frightened, Debby sat in her vehicle for a moment, asking the Lord what to do.

Returning to the house, she placed a call to Lew and Lillian Price. Lew and Lillian had known the Keims for years, and also knew Debby and Sandi, who sometimes called them from Maryland to check on Bill and Harriet. When Lew answered his phone that morning, sometime after 8:00 am, he was shocked to learn from Debby that her mother was missing. Lew told her he'd be right over and then he and Lillian quickly got dressed and drove the three miles to the Keim house.

"I've looked all over the house," Debby said, "and I can't find mom anywhere."

Lew knew that Harriet liked going over to the blueberry patch and also enjoyed walking out behind her house where paths had been cut through the heavy brush. Lew instructed Debby to go search the berry patch, and said he'd take his truck down behind the house and drive through the paths. When neither search netted any results, Lew Price immediately called 911.

For some reason, the 911 call was initially dispatched to a different county, and it took a little while to straighten out the glitch. Finally, however, the Pennsylvania State Police (PSP) at Gibson, took the missing person report on Harriet Keim. Lew gave the dispatcher a description of Harriet and told them what Debby said she was last wearing; a pair of red-striped pajamas.

While he made the call for help, Debby went back inside to do a more thorough search of the house. But after Lew hung up the phone, he turned to see an upset Debby coming towards him carrying a pair of red-striped pajamas. She had found them neatly folded in her mother's dresser drawer; Debby said. Apparently, Harriet Keim had changed before she disappeared.

Although Debby didn't live with her parents and had little knowledge of the clothes her mother owned, she soon realized that what Harriet had been wearing the day before was also missing. A pair of blue jeans, a caramel colored sweater with embroidered flowers on the front, slip on loafers with blue tassels, her wedding rings, her watch, and a small green purse with long straps. Debby didn't believe her mother had worn a coat, however because it appeared that all of her outerwear was accounted for.

Lew asked Debby to find phone numbers for everyone living nearby, and then left to drive to the church parish located a mile away. He knew the church was the last place Harriet had seen Bill, and he thought she might have walked there looking for him. On the way, he stopped by Carl Stahl's farm and told him about the disappearance. Carl owned a private plane and promised to take it out for an aerial search as soon as the fog lifted.

While the two men talked, a state trooper car flew by and turned down Airport Road, headed towards the Keim's. By the time Lew checked the church and returned to the house, there were already three state troopers there talking to Debby.

In the meantime, Carl Stahl had contacted another neighbor, Julie Ray*, who immediately drove up to the Keim house, arriving around 9:45. She offered to take her four-wheeler out to look for the missing woman but realized she needed to get gas for it first. Leaving the Keims, she drove to a convenient store/gas station, stopping at several places along the way to line up people to participate in a search.

For the small area where the Keims lived, the response to Harriet's disappearance was incredible. Not only did the police show up, but so did the fire company, the American Red Cross, EMT's, and scores of volunteers. By 10:30 am the nearby woods were teeming with searchers, both on foot and ATV's, and by later that afternoon, the canine units had begun to arrive as well.

Everyone was optimistic that the missing woman would soon be found. At most, the window of opportunity for Harriet to have disappeared seemed to be little more than an hour and a half. Debby had seen her mother at 6:00 am, and discovered her missing at 7:30. If Harriet had wandered into the woods, it seemed impossible that she could have gotten far. The foliage was thick, and the ground covered by mounds of fallen leaves that left rocks, branches and holes completely invisible. Even those who were young and agile found it difficult to walk, their search constantly hampered by these hidden objects that caused them to stumble and repeatedly fall. It seemed clear that an eighty-four-year-old woman would not have been able to negotiate such rugged terrain.

While the intensive search was going on, Debby's phone rang, and she recognized her father's number. Bill was calling from the hospital and had not yet been informed of his wife's disappearance. Debby feared what the news might do to him, but Bill took it calmly, perhaps believing himself that it wouldn't be long before she was found. Later that day doctors released Bill from the hospital, and Lew and Lillian Price drove the twenty miles to Scranton to bring him home. There, he and his two daughters, Debby and Sandi, who had also arrived at her parents' house that afternoon, sat down to pray for Harriet's safe return.

Despite the massive effort, no trace of Harriet Keim was found that day. And as daylight faded into dusk, and then to complete darkness, those who had come out with such high hopes of finding the missing woman, reluctantly abandoned the search for the night.

~*~*~

By dawn on Wednesday, October 1, 2014, Harriet had been gone for twenty-four hours, and searchers were once again in the woods looking for her. Everyone, it seemed, wanted to help. The Red Cross was there, dishing out food donated by local restaurants, bars and delis, all free of charge. The Emergency Management Agency helped organize volunteers who arrived by the carload, many of them having called off work to help with the search. More than one canine unit was also there, the dog's handlers leading them through brush so thick that even fully clothed, the thorns and pickers ripped and tore at the searcher's skin.

Debby was staying with Julie Ray, and the two women were up early, walking Airport Road and calling out Harriet's name. It was while they searched that Julie suddenly remembered something she hadn't thought about before; Julie Ray had a video surveillance camera mounted to her house. Could the camera have picked up anything from the morning before, she wondered?

Hurrying home, Julie re-wound the tape to 6:00 am on the morning of September 30, and then sat back to watch. Although her camera was a decent system, it wasn't top of the line; it didn't record anything when it was dark, and what it did pick up wasn't crystal clear. But it did show some activity from the morning of September 30, 2014.

The first image to flash across the screen was a vehicle that drove down Airport Road at exactly 7:02 am. The picture was grainy, however, and although the vehicle looked like an SUV, it was impossible to tell for sure. At 7:55 am, Debby's white Jeep appeared on the screen, also driving down Airport Road, and then returned at 8:06 am. The next vehicle to appear came up the road at 8:47 am, but the make and model were indiscernible. Three minutes later, at 8:50 am, what looked like a white SUV drove down the road. Six minutes after that, the Herrick Township truck was seen coming up the road, and at 9:24, another truck, (possibly Lew and Lillian Price), also came up the road. Only four minutes later, another white SUV went down the road, and the next vehicle seen was Julie Ray's, at 9:33 am as she drove up to the Keim house. There was no sign of Harriet on the tape, no image of anyone walking along the road, and nothing that could be considered suspicious.

Two other residents of Airport Road told investigators that they too had driven past Julie's house that morning; one of them at 6:00 am, and the other at 7:00, and neither saw Harriet Keim or anyone else. Both admitted, however, that it was difficult to see anything that morning due to the fog; which, they said, was "thick as pea soup."

If Harriet Keim walked in front of Julie Ray's house that morning, it had to have been while it was still dark out.

That same afternoon, the volunteers in the woods began doing a line search shoulder to shoulder while others probed a swampy area behind the Keim house. Volunteers were using ATV's and four-wheel drive vehicles to look for the missing woman, and some even came out on horseback. Carl Stahl had taken his plane up the day before, and now helicopters were brought in to do their own aerial search.

The search for Harriet Keim was intense, professional and well organized. Coordinators set up huge maps, marking out the territory for each group to search. Old, hand-dug wells, common in the area, all had their depths probed. Vacation homes, used mainly in winter for ski enthusiasts, were also checked, but no one found a thing.

On Thursday, a drone was flown over the area, and dive teams began searching the many ponds and waterways that dotted the landscape. More dogs were also brought in, including a team out of Eagle Creek, New York, and one from Calvert County, Maryland.

Ironically, Debby's husband, Steve, was part of the Calvert County Search and Rescue Team back home, and the dog Debby had with her in Pennsylvania was a member of that canine unit. Steve, however, was the dog's handler, and she responded only to him in a search situation. Because of this, Debby had not been able to use her dog to search. Her husband was out of the country and wouldn't return until Saturday, October 4, but Calvert County, realizing the need of one of their own, responded by sending four of their own searchers and three of their dogs to Pennsylvania to help.

Despite all of their intensive efforts, not a single thing was found on Thursday. Nothing.

~*~*~

As the search continued on Friday, the police received their first alleged sighting of Harriet Keim since she disappeared. Someone had reportedly seen the eighty-four-year-old woman at a CVS drugstore in the city of Berwick, nearly 70 miles away. Both her family, and those searching for her were hopeful, but it was quickly determined that the woman at the CVS was not Harriet Keim.

By now, authorities and searches alike were beginning to feel uneasy. They had found absolutely nothing that would help them determine what had happened to Harriet Keim. Something should have been found—her purse, one of her slip on loafers, a piece of her sweater snagged on a link of barbed wire—something, anything. Even more worrying was the fact that the next day, October 4, 2014, was the start of bow hunting season in Northeast Pennsylvania, and the search would have to be suspended

As things turned out, that first day of hunting season would not only suspend the search for Harriet Keim, but essentially end it for good. Although Debby's husband would take their dog out and search on his own, and Eagle Creek would send their dogs again—this time cadaver dogs—after October 4, the intensive, organized search was basically over.

People had searched for Harriet Keim for four days, covering an entire three mile radius in their quest to find her. Her photo had been shown on local news stations and television. Missing posters bearing her picture littered the area. A facebook page was set up and regularly added to. Yet despite all these efforts, not one clue to indicate what had happened to her was ever found.

It seemed obvious that Harriet Keim did not just wander away. The terrain was simply too rugged for her to traverse. She would have become exhausted; would have fallen or hurt herself, or, at the very least, left some type of evidence to show where she had been. Another thing that indicates that Harriet Keim did not just wander away is the fact that with all the search dogs brought in, not one of them picked up the missing woman's scent. Not one.

When Harriet Keim disappeared that morning, she did not have a coat or her medication; most specifically, her anti-seizure drugs. According to her doctor, if that medicine were stopped abruptly, it could produce, "severe seizures, blackouts, and a rise in blood pressure." As far as is known, Harriet has not had this medication since September 29, 2014.

There have been virtually no tips or sightings of the missing woman either. Other than the early tip from the CVS in Berwick, there has only been one other sighting that initially gave the family hope. This one came from the Pine Grove area; a place Harriet is familiar with, and one that has been in the news recently because of the search for alleged cop killer Eric Frein. A clerk in a convenient store identified Harriet as a woman who came in to buy a pretzel and a soda, but it has since been determined that the woman was not Harriet.

So what happened to Harriet Keim? There are numerous theories of course, but what most people agree on is that she didn't just wander away. Initially, a few people had suggested that she may have encountered a wild animal, but this seems unlikely. Something would have been found if she had—broken foliage, blood, her shoes or her purse. While animals might drag a body off, they don't take them miles and miles away, and hide them so they can never be found. If Harriet had been attacked by a bear or a coyote, some indication of it would have been noticed, and her body undoubtedly found.

It seems clear that Harriet Keim is no longer in the area and that someone took her away. But who, and for what reason? And is foul play involved?

Could someone have abducted the elderly woman when they saw her alone in the dark on that early Tuesday morning? Harriet did have her purse with her, and although it's unknown how much money she had, it could have been anywhere up to $100 or more. A paltry sum, indeed, but people have robbed—and killed—for much less. The idea that Harriet Keim became the victim of an unknown predator cannot be discounted.

There's also the possibility that Harriet was accidentally hit by a car and the driver, for some unknown reason, took her body to conceal the crime. It was foggy that morning, and Harriet may have been walking on the road when it was still dark. If someone came speeding around a bend, they might not have seen her until it was too late. If they had been drinking, or driving without a license or something of that nature, they may have panicked and decided to get rid of the body. Although that could have happened, there's no evidence that it did—no broken glass or vehicle parts on the road, and no reports of anyone in the area with fresh damage to their car.

It's also been suggested that Harriet might have flagged down a passing motorist on her own and asked the driver for a ride. She could have said her husband was in the hospital, and she needed to get there, and there are few people who wouldn't want to help a little old lady.

This is a possibility since descriptions of how severe Harriet's dementia was vary. Bill Keim and his daughters say that Harriet could appear lucid, but within a few minutes of speaking to her it would become obvious that something was wrong. Lew and Lillian Price agree with that assessment; saying that Harriet's dementia would be clear to anyone she encountered.

Elliot Ross, however, another friend of the Keims, and one who has known Harriet for thirty years, says that unless you knew her, you would think she was perfectly fine. Elliot described Harriet as a very social person who could carry on a normal conversation with no problem.

So I suppose it is possible that someone gave Harriet a ride on that Tuesday morning, perhaps not realizing that there was anything wrong. But this scenario has its own set of problems.

If someone did pick Harriet up and innocently gave her a ride, why hasn't the driver come forward to report it? Airport Road is a desolate dirt road unknown to most everyone except those who live in the area. The chances of anyone other than a local being on that road are fairly slim. The disappearance was not only publicized but has been the talk of the area for the past month. Surely anyone local who picked her up would know that.

But even if it wasn't a local who picked her up, even if it was a stranger who dropped her off and doesn't know she's missing, why hasn't she been found where he left her? Harriet has been gone for almost an entire month now, and there has been no reported activity on any of her credit cards or bank accounts. Surely, whatever money she carried in that small, green purse is long gone by now. How is she eating? Where is she sleeping? Fliers bearing her picture have been posted around the state, and hospitals have been called and checked. Yet there have been no reports of sightings of her.

The disappearance of Harriet Keim is a true mystery, riddled with unanswered questions. What happened to her? Where is she? Who was driving the different vehicles seen on Julie Ray's surveillance camera and which have yet to be identified?

From all descriptions, Harriet Keim is a kind and gentle soul, friendly, soft-spoken, and very loving. She needs to be found, and her family needs to know what happened to her.

Please take a close look at the missing poster in the picture section of this book. Harriet is described as:

A WHITE FEMALE, 84 YEARS OLD, 5' 1" TALL, 100 POUNDS, SLIGHT BUILD, PALE COMPLEXION, WITH GREEN EYES AND GREY/SILVER SHOULDER LENGTH HAIR. LAST SEEN WEARING A CARAMEL COLORED SHIRT WITH EMBROIDERED FLOWERS ON FRONT, BLUE JEANS, LOAFERS WITH BLUE TASSLES, AND CARRYING A GREEN PURSE.

ANYONE WITH INFORMATION SHOULD CALL 911 OR THE PENNSYLVANIA STATE POLICE AT 570-465-3151.

The Keim family would like to thank the community and everyone who has helped and supported them in this most trying time. Although room does not permit those people to be individually named, each is known to the family, and they are eternally grateful to all of them.

Postscript: On November 13, 2014, the body of Harriet Keim was found in a wooded area not far from her home. As of this date, no information regarding how she died has been released.

Made in the USA
Middletown, DE
31 May 2015